D1264060

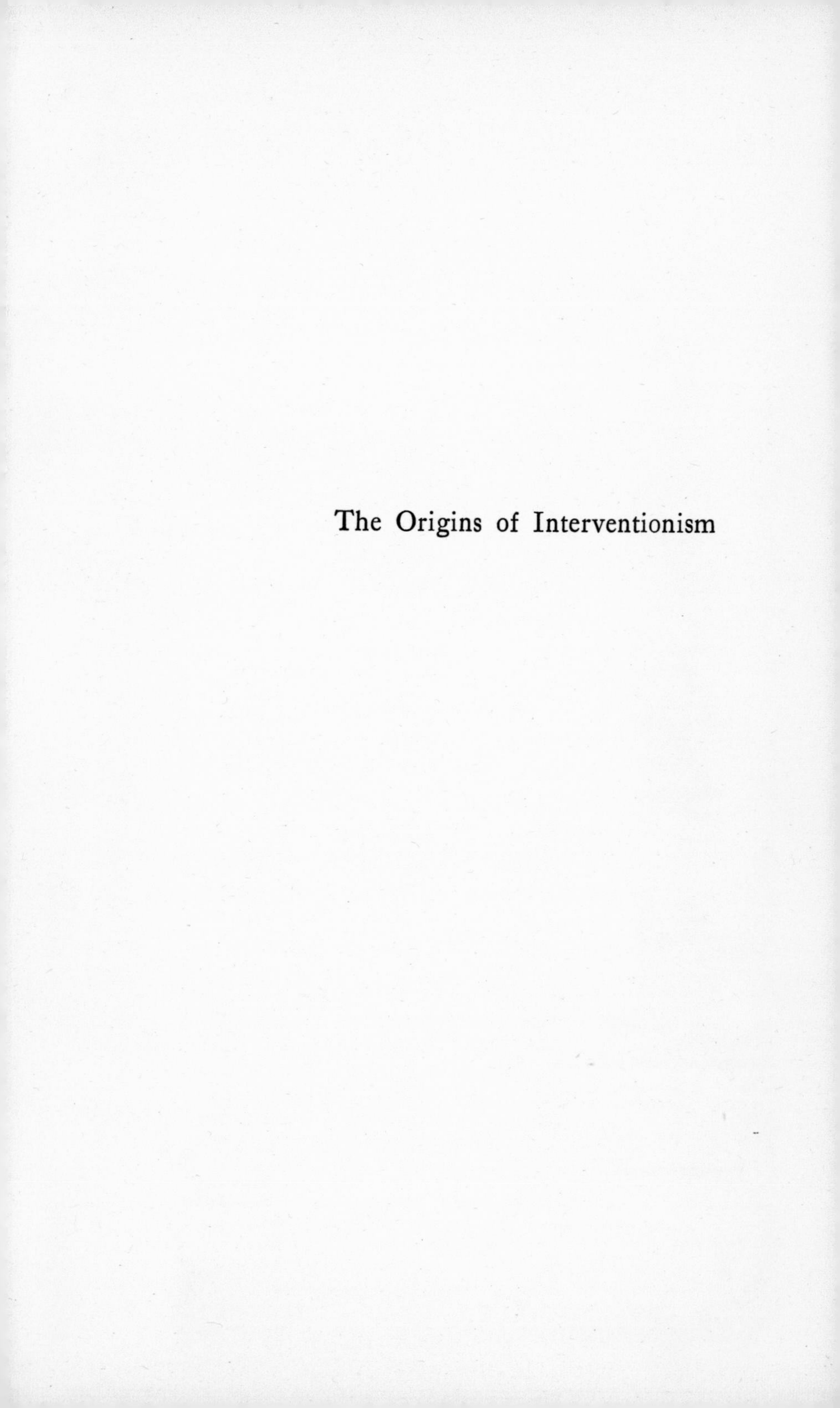

The Origins of Interventionism

The Origins of Interventionism

The United States and the Russo-Finnish War

by

ROBERT SOBEL

BOOKMAN ASSOCIATES, NEW YORK

Library of Congress Catalog Card Number: 60-14918

Manufactured in the United States of America

To

H. B. P.

ACKNOWLEDGMENTS

The importance of ideology in foreign relations was first introduced to me by Professor Henry B. Parkes of New York University, and it was he who suggested that this book be written. Many of my colleagues at Hofstra College contributed their knowledge and insights during its conception. The gentle prodding and encouragement of Professors Gerrit P. Judd, Robert Davison, John Marcus and Linton Thorn, who read and re-read large sections of the book, are greatly appreciated. In the gathering of material the staffs of the Franklin D. Roosevelt Library and the Library of Congress were most helpful. Mrs. Olga O'Brian undertook the tedious job of typing the final manuscript, and my wife quietly suffered through the labor of an author with a book aborning.

Hofstra College, 1960

CONTENTS

Chapter One

THE ISOLATIONIST BACKGROUND

Toward the end of 1939, after months of negotiations in Helsinki and Moscow, the Soviet Union attacked Finland. One hundred days later the fighting ended. Now almost forgotten in this country, the Winter War crowded World War II off the headlines for three important months. It precipitated a "great debate" in Congress and stirred the nation deeply.

This book is a study of how the conflict changed American attitudes toward foreign affairs. More specifically, it deals with the impact of the War upon American isolationism.

Most Americans were isolationists between the two World Wars. They interpreted statements of Washington, Jefferson and Monroe to mean that America was unique, and had a destiny distinct from that of Europe. Isolationists believed that the old continent was a place of evil intrigue, from which their forefathers had fled to find a better life. "Europe is immoral," they said, and they considered the World War to have been a conflict of rival imperialisms which should not have concerned the United States. The essential dishonesty of the Allies was proven when they reneged on their war debts. "Never again," said the isolationists, and they refused to join the League of Nations, washed their hands of international intrigue, and prepared to re-enter the nineteenth century by electing Warren Harding to the presidency.

A small minority remained internationalist. They believed, with Woodrow Wilson, that peace was indivisible, and that the United States had to take its rightful place as arbiter of that peace. "We are bound to the old world by ties of language, custom and tradition," said the internationalists. In addition, Europe was an important market for American goods, and the United States in turn needed material produced in Europe or in her colonies. The internationalists observed that Washington had delivered his farewell message at a time when the oceans were effective barriers behind which the nation could take refuge. This was no longer true when aircraft crossed the oceans regularly in a matter of hours. If the isolationist spoke of the dream of a new civilization unaffected by European squabbles, the internationalist envisaged a congress of like-minded countries, guided by the United States, whose experience would serve as a model and inspiration to all. Both were ardent patriots, but the internationalist and isolationist had differing dreams of the future.

Both philosophies can be found in the early career of Franklin D. Roosevelt, whose years in the Navy Department during World War I marked his first contact with foreign affairs. Like many of his contemporaries, F.D.R. fell heir to the internationalism of Woodrow Wilson. Roosevelt's support of Wilson and the League was a major factor in his being nominated for the vice-presidency in 1920. But F.D.R. was not a simon pure Wilsonian; he did not share the President's belief that the global struggle had been a war to end all wars. During the campaign he stated that the United States must remain on guard against future conflicts. Although this talk was unpopular at a time when the nation was trying to forget the bloodshed of 1917-18, he stated that threats of new wars could not be ignored. On one occasion Roosevelt went so far as to advocate the then politically impossible system of compulsory military training.[1] A close reading of F.D.R.'s speeches at this time show him almost as a believer of what would later be described as the "Fortress America" concept.

The Democratic defeat did not shake Roosevelt's determination to keep America on a military par with other nations. In commenting on the disarmament pacts he wrote that "war cannot be outlawed by resolution alone." In 1923 he indicated his willingness to scrap the League and substitute in its place a "Society of Nations" which the United States could join without becoming involved in European affairs. In F.D.R.'s proposed organization each member state would have the right to join in regional associations and to withdraw from any matter in which it felt itself not to be involved.[2] The nation was overwhelmingly isolationist, and Roosevelt adjusted his stand to meet the times. During the post-war decade he stressed the progressive aspect of his Wilsonian heritage and minimized its internationalist side. So successful was he in this that by 1932 Roosevelt had emerged as a bearer of the Democratic Party's reform tradition and its best hope for the presidency. As such he wooed the western progressive wing of the party. After convincing William Randolph Hearst and others of this group that his internationalism was a thing of the past, Roosevelt won the nomination. On the eve of the election which would take him into the White House, F.D.R. took an isolationist-progressive stance.[3] Internationalists bemoaned this apparent about-face. When Roosevelt won the convention's endorsement, some refused to support this man "who stood with Wilson in 1920 for the League of Nations and the new internationalism" and who had now "gone over to the nationalists and isolationists." [4] The internationalists were disenchanted, but the isolationists worked for Roosevelt in 1932.[5]

Whether dictated by political considerations or by a sincere belief that the United States should remain aloof from international engagements, Roosevelt's isolationism was to be built into the early New Deal. Politics played an important part in this wedding of recovery and reform at home and isolation from foreign influences. F.D.R. had been elected by an overwhelming margin, but he had no way of knowing whether the nation had voted for him or against Hoover. Could a program of relief and reform be carried out without the aid of important Republicans, who might control the Senate after the 1934 election? This question must have crossed F.D.R.'s mind as he entered the White House. He courted leading Republicans in the hope of using them to construct a progressive front with which he could challenge the conservative alliance of southern Democrats and northern Republicans. Roosevelt succeeded; he formed a coalition which was to last for five years—a coalition which united the Republican tradition of Theodore Roosevelt with the Democratic tradition of Woodrow Wilson. The foremost isolationists in Congress became charter members of this group. As La Follette and T.R. had opposed the League, so their intellectual and political legatees in the Republican

Party insisted that F.D.R. reject internationalism. The progressive Republicans—sometimes known as "the sons of the wild jackass"—became an important part of the Roosevelt alliance. Isolationist Democrats provided Roosevelt with the needed margin in winning the nomination and election, and isolationist Republicans gave vital support to the early New Deal.

Perhaps the most distinguished member of the isolationist-progressive-Republican faction was William Borah of Idaho. His career was typical of those of many of his progressive colleagues. Borah consistently crossed party lines in order to support bipartisan liberal measures. From the time he entered the Senate in 1907 until his death in 1939 he steered an independent course which won him the support of Democrats as well as Republicans in his home state. Borah was one of the earliest progressives. During his first year in the Senate he had been a leader in the fight for a federal income tax and the direct election of senators. The cornerstone of his philosophy was that any and all legislation which would bring government closer to the people should be supported regardless of any other consequences. Americans were unique, he said, and must be purified internally and protected against deleterious foreign influences. To Borah this meant England; he maintained that Great Britain dragged the United States into war in 1917, not only killing thousands of Americans and depleting the nation's resources but also interrupting the progressive crusade. During the twenties he had called for a renewal of reform, but the nation was quite satisfied with the New Era. Borah criticized both parties for their stagnation, and turned to foreign affairs for his "new crusade." He had led the opposition to Wilson in 1919, and now he opposed all contacts with the former allies of that period. When Harding and Coolidge, neither of whom could be considered internationalist, suggested that America could not secede from the planet, however desirable such an action might be, Borah charged that the State Department had become nothing but a British Embassy, "and the British know it." [6] On the other hand, Borah was willing to join hands with those nations which had escaped from the European orbit as had the United States. For example, he favored the recognition of the Soviet Union. Borah believed that Stalin was attempting to better the lives of the average Russian in much the same fashion as the progressives had done for the average American. "They have a future," said this man who disdained the European past. "Their face is toward better things." Statements of this order earned for Borah the title of "Russia's unofficial ambassador to the United States." [7]

Borah became a leader of those progressive Republicans who supported Roosevelt on domestic issues while at the same time he helped to sway the early New Deal to isolationism. His group, which included Hiram Johnson, "Young Bob" La Follette, Arthur Capper, Henrick Shipstead, Charles McNary, Gerald Nye and George Norris, was highly respected and talented. They had a common geographic background—all came from the midwest and far west—and all had earned the label of "progressive." On important occasions they tended to vote together. As such, they supported social security, public utilities expansion, pro-labor legislation and other reform measures as well as the Roosevelt program in the field of banking and currency. If the President wished to preserve this favorable coalition he would have to tread lightly in the field of foreign affairs. In 1933, however, the reformers of both parties were united in support of reform and isolation. Later on, when the isolationist-progressive-Republicans voiced their support of neutrality legislation which was more restrictive than that which F.D.R. desired, the President was able to salve his conscience by setting the gains in the matter of recovery and reform against the seemingly minor setbacks in the field of presidential discretion in foreign relations.[8] Then too, many of these Republicans—the most important of whom were Norris, La Follette and Johnson—had supported Roosevelt in 1932, thus endangering their political futures. F.D.R. owed them a debt of gratitude which, if paid, might help to bring the west into the Democratic Party. Roosevelt's devotion to the isolationist cause seemed genuine, and he continued this policy during the beginnings of pre-war activity in Europe in the thirties. Less than a month after the outbreak of the Italo-Ethiopian War, Roosevelt won their approval when he stated that the twin objectives of the New Deal were "the application of intelligence and good will to the solution of our domestic problems and the avoidance of foreign entanglements."[9]

This program enabled F.D.R. to attract progressives of both parties to the New Deal banner, but it also served to alienate many conservative-internationalist-Democrats. One such individual who remained in the Roosevelt camp despite grave misgivings at times was Cordell Hull, the Secretary of State. Hull entered the Tennessee legislature at the age of twenty-two, later on served in the Spanish-American War, and was elected to the House of Representatives in 1907, the same year Borah entered the Senate. From that time until the end of World War II—almost forty years—he was a potent force in Democratic politics. Though never closely associated with Wilson during the New Freedom days, he had supported him on the question of American entry into World War I. After this initial immersion into international affairs, Hull grew in stature until, by 1933, he represented that segment of the Democratic Party which was generally conservative on domestic change and which accepted an international role for the nation. Although both of these positions were out of harmony with the early New Deal, Hull was named to the cabinet in order to placate those Democrats who feared Roosevelt's novel economic theories. Always aware of propriety, Hull never attempted to impose his ideas on domestic questions on the President, although he could not hide his dislike of the "brain trust." However, he fought every attempt on the part of that group to encroach on his preserve.

Hull was an ardent believer in low tariffs, which he considered to be the key to peace and good will between nations. A throwback to nineteenth century liberalism, but for the question of the tariff he might have found himself more at home with Hoover than with F.D.R. As a member of the Roosevelt cabinet he pressed for his ideals in the twentieth century world, and objected when the President promised to spare no effort to restore world trade by international economic readjustment only *after* internal affairs were set aright.[10] Hull fought devaluation of the dollar, on the ground that it would adversely affect international trade. Identified with that group which believed that international recovery was a prerequisite to domestic prosperity, Hull travelled to London soon after taking office in order to participate in the economic conferences designed to cure the depression through concerted efforts by all nations. Roosevelt's unwillingness to follow his program was irksome to Hull, but even more serious was the interference of Assistant Secretary Raymond Moley, who tried to block him at every turn and at times acted as though he, and not Hull, was the chief architect of American foreign policy. When Moley's interference began, Hull threatened to resign, and it took every bit of Roosevelt's persuasiveness and charm to avert his leaving the cabinet.[11] Hull remained, eventually to serve in his post longer than any other secretary of state in history. Throughout this tenure his position was constantly endangered by New Dealers who attempted to replace him or lessen his influence. Hull outlasted most of them, but not because he was able to convince F.D.R. of the soundness of his position. He was needed to placate the conservative-internationalist-Democrats as Borah was needed to do the same for the progressive-isolationist-Republicans. Roosevelt kept both in his coalition, but neither had the power he desired. Roosevelt was throughout his career his own domestic and foreign secretaries.

NOTES

Chapter I: THE ISOLATIONIST BACKGROUND

1 Frank Freidel, *Franklin D. Roosevelt: The Ordeal* (Boston, 1954), pp. 17-18.

2 Selig Adler, *The Isolationist Impulse: Its Twentieth Century Reaction* (New York, 1956), p. 200.

3 Franklin D. Roosevelt, "Our Foreign Policy: A Democratic View" (*Foreign Affairs,* Vol. 6, No. 4, July, 1928), p. 585; James Farley, *Behind the Ballots: The Personal History of a Politician* (New York, 1938), pp. 101-3 ff.

4 *The Nation,* Vol. 134, No. 10, February 17, 1932, p. 182.

5 Charles A. Beard, *American Foreign Policy in the Making, 1932-1940* (New Haven, 1946), pp. 83-85.

6 William K. Hutchinson, *News Articles on the Life and Works of Hon. William E. Borah,* 76th Congress, 3rd Session, *Senate Document No. 150* (Washington, 1940), p. 43.

7 Ray Tucker and Frederick R. Barkley, *Sons of the Wild Jackass* (Boston, 1932), p. 11; William E. Borah, *Bedrock* (Washington, 1936), p. 51.

8 Foster Rhea Dulles, *America's Rise to World Power* (New York, 1955), pp. 176-77.

9 Raymond Moley, *After Seven Years* (New York, 1939), p. 319.

10 *New York Times,* March 5, 1933.

11 Cordell Hull, *Memoirs* (New York, 1948), I, 256-69.

Chapter II

ROOSEVELT, NYE AND NEUTRALITY

One of the isolationists' most important sources of strength was the public belief that American participation in the World War was a mistake. There was a widespread feeling that the nation had been duped by the pro-British Wilson and House, whose sins were compounded by their ineptness in diplomacy and the adroitness of their British and French opposite numbers. It was further believed that the machinations of international bankers, led by J. P. Morgan, had prompted the Administration to sever relations with the Central Powers and eventually had led the nation to war. Finally, the munitions makers were considered the most despicable of the lot. They operated, so the public thought, by fomenting wars in an attempt to wring profits from both sides.[1] None of these attitudes was new. Anglophobia was as old as the nation itself and the anti-big business sentiments of the progressive era were not entirely forgotten. Indeed, the stock market crash and the depression seemed to call for a new crusade against the malefactors of great wealth. The animosity toward the munitions makers is illustrative of the search for a "devil theory" to explain unfortunate experiences in American history.[2]

At this time the first rumblings of the National Socialist revolution in Germany were heard as were the beginnings of a new arms race in Europe. The American people, remembering the lessons of 1917, showed an overwhelming desire to steer clear of new entanglements. A flood of books and magazine articles appeared which purported to "tell the real truth" about the international traffic in arms and other implements of war; of how innocent people had been sent to their death by a few people in high places of influence.[3] A new group of revisionist writers claimed that the ties between the bankers, the arms manufacturers and the Government had not been severed after the World War; if anything, the "merchants of death" had an important voice in Washington which gave them the power to dictate policy.[4] Motion pictures appeared which reflected a strong anti-war bias, which intimated that bloodshed was meaningless and even criminal.[5] The stage was set for a new purge.

In March of 1934, *Fortune* published an article entitled "Arms and the Men."[6] It met with wide acclaim among the isolationist-progressives who, led by Borah, began to use it as a text for their anti-internationalist speeches.[7] Roosevelt also showed an interest in the article, which demonstrated that large profits had been made by some concerns during the World War. In a special message to Congress on May 18, Roosevelt recommended the establishment of a commission to study the *Fortune* charges. He said that many of the problems which caused the depression were due in no small measure to the uncontrolled activities of the manufacturers and merchants of "engines of destruction."[8] Soon thereafter the Democratic Party called for international control of munitions manufacturers, while the Republicans asked for nationalization of the industry. Both agreed that action against the arms makers was needed.[9]

If F.D.R. hoped to claim the issue for his own, the special message came too late; the progressive-isolationists had already begun their crusade. In February—a month before the *Fortune* article had appeared—Senators Gerald Nye of North Dakota and Arthur Vandenberg of Michigan had introduced a resolution to set up a committee to investigate the munitions industry.

The Nye-Vandenberg motion and the *Fortune* article were a striking instance of the right man getting the right issue at the right time. Nye had the article reprinted in the *Congressional Record* and adopted its arguments.[10] Led by Nye, the Senate speedily approved the motion for a special committee.[11] Due to a series of misunderstandings complicated by political chicanery, the Republican senator was named chairman of the committee which, had precedent been followed, would normally have been headed by a Democrat.[12]

Nor was this the only victory for the isolationist-progressives. The personnel of the committee reflected the extent of their success. The three Republican members ranged from Nye, the rabid isolationist, through Vandenberg, the mild isolationist, to W. Warren Barbour of New Jersey, who was relatively uninterested in foreign affairs but leaned toward isolationism. The most important Democrat in terms of interest and activity was Bennett Champ Clark of Missouri, who was intent on following in his father's footsteps and punishing his father's enemies. He felt that Wilson and Bryan had conspired to cheat the elder Clark of the Democratic presidential nomination in 1912, and his son singled them out for retribution. Wilson was dead, but his reputation could be tarnished so as to assure him a dark page in

American history. The fact that Clark was an ardent isolationist gave him intellectual justification for this action; he was operating in the name of principles, not merely attacking personalities. Nye welcomed Clark's nomination to the committee and called upon him for support on several crucial occasions.[13]

The other Democrats, though not so isolationist as Clark, were by no means internationalists. One of them, Walter George of Georgia, was so strongly opposed to the New Deal that he was singled out to be a "purge" victim in 1938. Homer T. Bone of Washington and James Pope of Idaho, the other members, were relatively unimportant. The former was an admirer of Charles McNary, the isolationist-progressive, while Pope lived under the shadow of the great Borah and accepted his dictates on almost every occasion. Thus, every member of the committee was of the isolationist persuasion and most could be counted upon to embarrass the internationalists whenever the opportunity presented itself.

From the first meeting, the committee captured the front pages. Representatives from such large arms firms as Curtiss-Wright and du Pont appeared and testified that they had sold and would sell their wares to almost anyone who paid the price. Lobbyists from other concerns admitted having "influenced" senators and congressmen as well as admirals and generals in their desire for profit.[14] The committee failed to implicate the munitions manufacturers in the fomenting of war, but Nye had demonstrated that a link did exist between them and elected federal officials. He implied that a few men in private concerns might easily involve the nation in war in order to line their own pockets. He suggested various means of correcting such abuses, including a bill which, if passed, would automatically impose an arms embargo on the nation in case of war.[15] He was seconded in this by Bernard Baruch, who suggested new legislation regulating federal contracts.[16]

The Nye Committee had captured the public imagination. Hollywood sensed this, and produced a "quickie" film entitled, *War Is a Racket,* which maintained that wars were "wittingly fomented by the munitions manufacturers."[17] Historians of both the isolationist and internationalist persuasion began to grind out works which directly or indirectly supported or attacked the "Nye mentality." Charles Seymour and Newton D. Baker wrote popular histories which attempted to vindicate the Wilsonians,[18] but they had little effect when compared to the works of leading isolationists like Walter Millis, whose *Road to War* made the best seller list and was backed by "Book-of-the-Month." Millis reinforced Nye's contention that Wilson's pro-Allied bias had forced war on an unwilling American nation. The author did not claim that his work was an authoritative study; in the preface he stated that it was "an effort in interpretation rather than research."[19] Millis attempted to show how an emotional partnership with the Allies soon led to an economic alliance which, in turn, led to a military pact. The book has several important faults and was criticized by many historians, but it was widely read and praised by the isolationists, who delighted in finding their views corroborated. Senator Bone said that "it was upon what this man (Millis) exposed so well in his book that I postulated my stand for a strong, mandatory, neutrality bill." The Senator waxed rhapsodic over the volume;

"the lamp of experience burns so brightly in his hands that we are convinced by his recital of the record." [20] *The Road to War* was on its way to becoming the handbook for the New Neutrality of the thirties.

The book came out as Nye and his colleagues were preparing to open the second round of hearings in 1936. During this session the banking fraternity made its appearance and attempted to justify its pro-Allied position prior to American entry into the World War. Thomas Lamont of the House of Morgan admitted his bias readily. "Like most of our contemporaries and friends and neighbors," he declared, "we wanted the Allies to win from the outset of the war." The Morgan group was "pro-Allied by inheritance, by instinct, by opinion" and favored American aid to Britain and France from 1914 onward.[21] Morgan was more direct. When asked whether he thought his firm had acted correctly in advocating aid to the Allies, he responded: "Certainly we did the right thing. We would do it again if we had to." [22]

This was the opportunity that Clark had waited for, and he did not let such statements pass without a response. He charged Lamont with influencing the Wilson Administration's foreign policy decisions, and suggested that Lamont himself had been an important factor in the American decision to intervene in 1917.[23] Everyone knew that the Morgan Bank had loaned large sums to the Allies, and if Clark could demonstrate that Wilson took the nation into war to protect these investments rather than to fight for the national interest, the former president would be discredited forever. Clark hinted at this; he accused Morgan and Company, "whether acting as agents of the British Government or on their own responsibility," of having been the prime mover in drawing the United States into war. Clark further insinuated that Wilson was not loath to work with the bankers at that time.[24] Nye did not seem perturbed at this line of inquiry especially since, as an isolationist Republican, he was attacking an internationalist Democrat. He was not prepared, however, for the torrent of criticism that descended upon him and Clark for their reckless statements. One periodical wrote: "Bennett Champ Clark precipitated one of the most venomous incidents in the recent history of Capitol Hill." [25] Senator Pope protested vigorously at the next meeting of the committee.

> The Chairman of this Committee is quoted in the press as making the charge that President Wilson and Secretary Lansing were falsifiers. Just what this has to do with an investigation of the munitions industry under the terms of the resolution is not possible to see. The purpose of the investigation is being lost sight of.[26]

With this, Pope and George walked out of the committee hearings. "We will take no part in such performance," said Pope.[27]

Other opposition was not long in coming. Tom Connally of Texas unleased an attack on Nye and Clark which was remarkable for its colorful figures of speech. He charged that "some checker-playing, beer-drinking back room of some low house is the only place for the . . . language of the Senator from North Dakota." Carter Glass, the 78 year old relic of Wilsonian days, rose to defend his former chief. He proclaimed that "any man who would asperse the integrity and veracity of Woodrow Wilson is a coward." Not in all his 35 years of service had he known such a "shocking exhibition . . . infamous libel . . . miserable demagogy." [28] Wilson must be avenged, and the best way to do this would be to shut off all appropriations for the Nye Committee. The Democrats presented a solid front in their refusal to vote additional funds, and by January 30 the investigations were doomed. Nye pleaded for the life of his committee. He argued that the group had not transcended the bounds of the motion which set it up, and that public interest demanded a continuance of its work. These entreaties fell on deaf ears; Nye had gone too far, and now had to pay for his errors. Sessions continued up to February 20, but as far as the public was concerned, they really had ended with the Clark blasts at Wilson. Nye and Clark had not proven their contention. There were no startling revelations at the hearings despite the publicity given them. But the munitions makers, the bankers, and the Wilson Administration had been tried by the press and radio, and had been found guilty. As is so often the case, people assumed that smoke meant fire, and spent the next four years in quenching or feeding a blaze that did not exist. Public opinion demanded that measures be taken to check those who worked behind the scenes, manipulated the strings and made statesmen hop to their every command. A movement was on foot to prevent profit making in time of war, and a poll of February 1, 1936, showed that all sections of the nation and members of both political parties agreed that the arms manufacturers should be "curbed." Seldom, if ever, had a clearer mandate been presented to the nation's legislators. Six months later the public was asked: "Do you favor governmental ownership of the munitions industry?" and 69% of the respondents answered in the affirmative.[29]

More important than the determination to curb the munitions makers was the growing distrust of presidential control of foreign affairs. Many isolationists believed that Clark had the goods on Wilson, and this was why the appropriations for the Nye Committee were stopped. They spoke and wrote of their belief, and found an audience in many quarters. This publicity set the stage for the final disintegration of the Wilsonian ideologies regarding the American Mission. Those who talked of "War for Democracy," "close collaboration with the European democracies" and the League of Nations were castigated.[30] The public was given a straw man by Nye and Clark; the President, whomever he may be, should not be given the power to deal away the lives and property of the nation without the direct consent of those involved. A strong president—such as F.D.R.—would have to be watched carefully to see that he did not overstep the bounds of his power.[31]

This attitude was immediately reflected in Congress. Before the investigations the legislature had approved Hull's reciprocal trade legislation, which to a great degree took the regulation of tariffs from their hands and made the President a co-partner in their control. Now Congress rejected Roosevelt's plan to bring the United States into the World Court.

The isolationist historians and publicists gloried in this atmosphere of caution and distrust, and they used the Nye reports as their text in spreading their messages. The ablest of this school wrote that the investigations were "comparable in significance to the diplomatic revelations that came in 1917 and the following years, when the secret archives of Petrograd, Berlin, and Vienna were torn open."[32] Hull spoke for many internationalists. "It is doubtful," he wrote, "that any Congressional committee has ever had a more unfortunate effect on our foreign relations unless it be the Senate Foreign Relations Committee considering the Treaty of Versailles submitted by President Wilson."[33] The majority of Americans were isolationist during the rest of the thirties, and the desire for neutrality forced a further retreat from Wilsonian idealism and internationalism. Perhaps this situation would have developed without the munitions investigations; the same people who applauded Nye in 1935 and 1936 elected F.D.R. on an isolationist platform in 1932 and, before that, had shown a reluctance to meddle in Europe during the twenties. What the Nye Committee did was to offer the isolationists a body of facts and testimony which served to jell the half-believed and half-suspected attitudes of the period. The influence of the committee was to be felt throughout the rest of this important decade and well into the first years of the next.

Nye's investigations coincided with the rise of dictatorships in Europe. While the du Ponts were being questioned about their profits in the first World War, Hitler prepared for the second by disregarding the Locarno pacts and re-occupying the Rhine. The dictator was arming for war, and some of his guns and planes were coming from the same American factories that had provided munitions for Europe in 1914.[34] Many Americans were alarmed; had not Nye shown that the munitions makers had a great influence in Washington? Might they not agitate for a new war which would bring them new profits? A plan must be devised to assure the nation that the pattern of 1914-1917 would not be repeated.

The Government had taken steps in this direction before Roosevelt and Hitler had become heads of their nations. In 1925 the United States ratified the Geneva Convention which would have forbidden the export of arms and munitions. Other nations had rejected the idea, which was forgotten for eight years.[35] Hoover revived the plan in 1933 when, as one of his last acts as President, he asked Congress to empower him to treat the Japanese aggressors in a different fashion than their Chinese victims. An embargo would be placed on the former nation, while arms would be sent to China. This plan was under consideration when F.D.R. entered the White House, and although the new President endorsed it and helped push the bill through the House, it was killed in the Senate Foreign Relations Committee.[36]

The idea of an embargo on arms was raised again in 1935, against the backdrop of war preparations and the Nye mentality. Neutrality legislation was introduced in both the House and Senate by the isolationists.[37] Most of these proposals would have bartered away freedom of the seas for a paper guarantee of freedom from European wars. The public seemed willing to make the exchange. Admiral Sims said that "we cannot keep out of war and at the same time enforce freedom of the seas." In the event of war, America must choose "between great profits with risk of war, on the one hand, or small profits with less risk on the other." Sims made it clear that he favored the second alternative. Nye expanded on this theme. We should make it clear to all Americans who deal with foreign nations that the flag does not follow the dollar. If the munitions makers sell to Europe, they must understand that their investments would not be safeguarded by Congress or the President. Nye also suggested that "it shall be illegal for the American flag to be flown upon any cargo destined for a country engaged in war." [38] Bone agreed; we should serve notice on Americans "that if they go into a war zone, they go at their own peril." [39] If our neutrality rights had been more clearly defined from 1914 to 1917, said Bernard Baruch, "we would have been less likely to have been drawn in, and might not have been drawn in." [40] In this spirit, Congress passed the Johnson Act, which withheld private loans from those nations that defaulted on their World War debts, and prepared to enact legislation which further restricted commerce with potential belligerants.

From 1935 to 1938 Congress passed and the President signed a series of neutrality acts which many felt would insulate the nation from foreign wars. There was an important difference of opinion, however, between F.D.R. and Congress as to what kind of legislation would be most effective. The Administration favored discretionary laws, which would allow the President wide liberties in applying embargoes. Congress, in the main, desired mandatory measures, ones which would apply automatically in time of war. Key Pittman, the Democratic Chairman of the Senate Foreign Relations Committee, was a staunch isolationist who opposed Roosevelt's attempts to gain a measure of latitude in foreign affairs.[41] Hull spoke for those in the [illegible]istration who believed that mandatory measures "[illegible]uld prevent our exercising our influence to prevent war." [42] Roosevelt was faced with the choice of fighting for freedom in foreign affairs or maintaining the isolationist-progressive coalition which had served him so well. If he chose to exert his influence to gain discretionary legislation, it might cripple the program of recovery and reform. Should he accept the isolationist-progressive position again, he would further compromise his standing with the Wilsonian internationalists. F.D.R. chose the second alternative. On March 20 he called the Nye Committee members to his offices and told them that he favored neutrality legislation "which would guarantee, in the event of a European war, the absolute neutrality of the American people." [43] Without Roosevelt's leadership the internationalists were helpless to fight against the Nye inspired Neutrality Act of 1935, which, in effect, forced the President to declare an arms embargo against all belligerents in case of war between two foreign nations.[44]

Hull was bitterly disappointed with the bill, which he felt would interfere with his actions as Secretary of State. Roosevelt also had misgivings, and admitted that "the inflexible provisions might draw us into war instead of keeping us out." [45] In a letter to William E. Dodd he expressed grave doubts as to whether or not his position in the controversy was sound. Roosevelt intimated that he would sponsor a stronger law in 1936, "leaving, however, some authority to the President." [46]

The weaknesses of the Neutrality Act showed themselves in its first application. When Roosevelt invoked it during the Italo-Ethiopian War, American businessmen sent a large quantity of non-military goods to Mussolini, who got all the planes, guns and tanks he needed from Germany. Since the Neutrality Act said nothing about non-military goods, such trade was within the letter, if not the spirit, of the law. Roosevelt moved to plug this loophole by declaring a moral embargo against Italy, but the trade continued.[47] Indeed, oil exports tripled and Italian purchases of manufactured goods from the United States doubled during the war.[48] Hull admitted that the moral embargo was a failure, and that the Neutrality Act would have to be re-written.[49] Nye agreed, but again insisted that Congress, and not the President, should be the senior partner in its application.

Once again Roosevelt sided with Nye and the isolationist-progressives. His public statements in favor of strict neutrality were as strong as those of any isolationist. Roosevelt told Congress that he had a twofold program of neutrality. First, he would oppose the attempts of any belligerent to obtain arms or munitions in the United States. In addition, he would forbid any belligerent from increasing its imports from this nation in time of war, thus preventing a repetition of the situation that developed during the Italo-Ethiopian War.[50] F.D.R. sponsored the Pittman-McReynolds bill in 1936, a document which made little attempt to increase presidential discretion.[51] Strict restrictions on loans and credits would automatically go into effect during foreign wars, and the President might even restrict foreign travel for American nationals. A munitions control board would supervise shipments of war goods, and American vessels would be forbidden to carry implements of war. Exports of non-military items would also be controlled by a board set up by the President.[52] Roosevelt was willing to surrender discretionary powers to Congress in regard to arms in return for a measure of discretion in the matter of non-military goods. Both sides seemed happy with this compromise. New Dealer Sol Bloom said that "as little power as possible in this matter should be left to presidential discretion" while conservative Professor Edwin Borchard of Yale added that "no man should have the power of regulating the entire foreign trade of the United States." [53]

With the support of both New Dealers and isolationist-progressives, passage of the Pittman-McReynolds bill was assured. The only grumbling came from the internationalists. Columnist Arthur Krock wrote that "once more, the isolationist viewpoint has established minority control of foreign policy" [54] and Hull later wrote that the only comfort he had received was the fact that the President was allowed the right to determine whether or not a state of war existed.[55] Roosevelt was delighted with the act. It was "a new and definitive step" in the direction of peace, and he extended its provisions to the Italo-Ethiopian War as soon as possible.[56]

With the passage of the 1936 Neutrality Act, Roosevelt became a leader of the isolationist movement. The bill was passed during an election campaign, and F.D.R. was too shrewd a politician to risk taking an unpopular stand at that time. All of his speeches which dealt with foreign policy in this campaign can be classed as isolationist. On August 14, he delivered the most important of these at Chautauqua. He stressed that fact that:

> We shun political commitments which might entangle us in foreign wars; we avoid connection with the political activities of the League of Nations. . . . We are not isolationists except insofar as we seek to isolate ourselves completely from war. . . . I have seen war. I have seen war on land and sea. I have seen blood running from the wounded. I have seen men coughing out their gassed lungs. I have seen the dead in the mud. I have seen cities destroyed . . . I have seen children starving. I have seen the agony of mothers and wives. I hate war.

Could Borah or Nye have put it better?

> I have spent unnumbered hours, I shall spend unnumbered hours thinking and planning how war may be kept from our nation. . . . I can at least make certain that no act of the United States helps to produce or to promote war.

But America must remain vigilant and on guard. Wars cannot be wished away, but must be defended against as the nation would defend itself against an actual aggressor.

> Yet, we must remember that so long as war exists on earth there will be some danger that even the nation which most ardently desires peace may be drawn into war.[57]

This one phrase notwithstanding, the Chautauqua speech was the most forceful isolationist utterance of the year. It estranged more internationalists, but it also won for F.D.R. the support of Gerald Nye, who campaigned for him in the 1936 election.[58]

NOTES

Chapter II: ROOSEVELT, NYE AND NEUTRALITY

1 Curtis MacDougall, *Understanding Public Opinion* (New York, 1952), pp. 95-96.

2 The best work on this subject is Richard Hofstadter, *The Age of Reform* (New York, 1957). Also, see Charles A. Beard, *The Devil Theory of War* (New York, 1936).

3 H.C. Englebrecht and F.C. Hanighen, *Merchants of Death* (New York, 1934); Seymour Waldman, *Death and Profits* (New York, 1934), are representative titles.

4 Guiles Davenport, *Zaharoff: High Priest of War* (Boston, 1934), attempted to demonstrate that a link existed between European and American munitions manufacturers, both of whom were dedicated to the fomenting of wars.

5 The most important of these were *All Quiet on the Western Front* and, later on, *They Gave Him a Gun.*

6 "Arms and the Men" (*Fortune,* Vol. 9, No. 3, March, 1934), pp. 113-26.

7 Borah, *Bedrock,* pp. 175-176.

8 *The Public Papers and Addresses of Franklin D. Roosevelt* (New York, 1938), III, 240.

9 *Fortune* (Vol. 13, No. 5, May, 1936), p. 26.

10 *Congressional Record,* 73rd Congress, 2nd Session, pp. 2192, 4323, 6688, 7154.

11 *New York Times,* April 13, 1934.

12 Hull, Memoirs, I, 398; Basil Rauch, *Roosevelt From Munich to Pearl Harbor* (New York, 1950), p. 24. James Byrnes, then in the Senate, claims that Democrats Clark and George were late in arriving at the organizational meeting, and that Bone voted for Nye as chairman. The vote would then have been four to one (Pope) for Nye. Had party discipline held, George would have become chairman. James F. Byrnes, *All in One Lifetime* (New York, 1958), pp. 89-90.

13 *New York Times,* January 19, 1936; Samuel W. Tait, Jr., "Champ Clark's Boy." (*The American Mercury,* Vol. 28, No. 109, January, 1933), p. 71.

14 United States Senate, Special Committee to Investigate the Munitions Industry, 73rd Congress, 3rd Session, *Hearings Before the Special Committee Investigating the Munitions Industry* (Washington, 1934-36), Pt. 9, pp. 2122, 2159-61; Pt. 18, pp. 4610-11; Pt. 21, pp. 5951-53; Charles and Mary Beard, *America in Midpassage* (New York, 1940), pp. 50-51.

15 *New York Times,* February 7, 1935.

16 *Munitions Investigations,* Pt. 22, pp. 6267-68, 6185; *New York Times,* December 14, 1934.

17 *New York Times,* December 10, 1934.

18 Charles Seymour, *American Diplomacy During the World War* (Baltimore, 1934); *American Neutrality, 1914-1917* (New Haven, 1935); Newton D. Baker, *Why We Went to War* (New York, 1936).

19 Walter Millis, *The Road to War* (New York, 1935), p. VII.

20 *Time* (Vol. 27, No. 8, February 24, 1936), p. 16.

21 *Munitions Investigations,* Pt. 25, p. 7505; Pt. 26, p. 7818; *Time* (Vol. 27, No. 3, January 20, 1936), p. 16; Walter Johnson, *The Battle Against Isolation* (Chicago, 1941), pp. 14-15.

22 *Munitions Investigations,* Pt. 26, p. 7847; Harold Hinton, *Cordell Hull: A Biography* (New York, 1942), p. 266.

23 *Time* (Vol. 27, No. 3, January 20, 1936), p. 16.

24 *Munitions Investigations,* Pt. 28, pp. 8581-83.

25 *Newsweek* (Vol. 7, No. 4, January 25, 1936), p. 12.

26 *Munitions Investigations,* Pt. 27, pp. 8633-34.

27 *Ibid., loc. cit.; New York Times,* January 27, 1936.

28 *Newsweek* (Vol. 7, No. 4, January 25, 1936), p. 13.

29 Hadley Cantril, *Public Opinion, 1935-1946* (Princeton, 1951), pp. 491-92.

30 Beard and Beard, *America in Midpassage,* p. 421.

31 An American Institute of Public Opinion poll on January 18, 1937, asked: "Should Congress or the President be mainly responsible for American neutrality policy?" 69% of those who answered said that Congress should have the control, while 31% favored presidential discretion. Cantril, *Public Opinion,* p. 966.

32 Beard, *Devil Theory of War,* p. 11.

33 Hull, *Memoirs,* I, 398.

34 A headline of the period read: "Reich Buys Planes Here for Air Force," *New York Times,* September 18, 1934.

35 "Efforts to Write a Permanent Neutrality Law" (*Congressional Digest,* Vol. 18, No. 10, October, 1939), p. 228.

36 Rauch, *Roosevelt From Munich to Pearl Harbor,* p. 20.

37 John Bassett Moore, "The New Isolationism" (*The American Journal of International Law,* Vol. 27, No. 4, October, 1933), p. 607.

38 Beard and Beard, *America in Midpassage,* pp. 429-30; mss. in New York Public Library.

39 *Munitions Investigations,* Pt. 22, pp. 6344-45.

40 *Ibid., loc. cit.*

41 *New York Times,* March 19, 1935.

42 Hull, *Memoirs,* I, 406.

43 John T. Flynn, *The Roosevelt Myth* (New York, 1948), p. 168.

44 United States Department of State, *Peace and War, United States Foreign Policy, 1931-1941* (Washington, 1943), pp. 266-71.

45 Hull, *Memoirs,* I, 404; *The Public Papers of Franklin D. Roosevelt,* IV, 345-46.

46 Elliott Roosevelt, ed., *F.D.R.: His Personal Letters, 1928-1945* (New York, 1950) III, 530-31.

47 Hull, *Memoirs,* I, 432-33; United States House of Representatives, Foreign Affairs Committee, 74th Congress, 2nd Session, *To Maintain the Neutrality of the United States in*

the Event of War Between or Among Foreign Nations (Washington, 1936), p. 17.

48 *Department of Commerce News Release,* November 23, December 21, 1935.

49 Hull, *Memoirs,* I, 435.

50 *The Public Papers of Franklin D. Roosevelt,* V, 11-12; *New York Times,* January 1, 3, 1936; "Establishing a Neutrality Policy for America" (*Congressional Digest,* Vol. 15, No. 1, January, 1936), pp. 3-4.

51 Hull, *Memoirs,* I, 463.

52 *New York Times,* January 6, 1936.

53 *To Maintain the Neutrality of the United States,* pp. 51-52, 79, 83.

54 *New York Times,* February 19, 1936.

55 Hull, *Memoirs,* I, 467.

56 *Peace and War,* p. 314.

57 *Roosevelt's Foreign Policy, 1933-1941* (New York, 1942), pp. 100-106.

58 Edgar E. Robinson, *They Voted for Roosevelt* (Stanford, 1947), p. 25.

Chapter III

THE GREAT DEBATE AND THE EMERGENCE OF INTERVENTIONISM

Roosevelt led the Democratic Party to its most spectacular electoral victory in 1936. Landon captured two states to F.D.R.'s 46; the Republican minority in the House fell to 88 and the G.O.P. Senate contingent to 16. Roosevelt's leadership was endorsed, but only because he had understood and followed the people's desire for peace and recovery. War came and went in Africa, was resumed in Asia, and showed signs of erupting in Europe. The world was soon to be engulfed in the greatest war of all time. Roosevelt knew this, but he also knew that one of the major reasons for his victory was the belief that a vote for him was a vote for isolationism. If the public wanted an isolationist president, Roosevelt would do his best to fill the bill. Hull opposed F.D.R. in this, and continued to advocate a greater amount of cooperation with the western democracies. In 1936 the two men seemed to be following different paths, and more than once the Secretary expressed his annoyance at the drift in American foreign policy. Roosevelt soothed Hull's ruffled feelings and retained him as Secretary of State. By keeping him in the cabinet, he was not only able to use Hull as a liaison with older Democrats who were skeptical of the New Deal, but he also left the door open for a possible future swing to internationalism.

Roosevelt and Hull did agree on one important issue in 1937: that of the Spanish Civil War. During this conflict, Hull supported Roosevelt's isolationism while some isolationists demanded intervention in the Spanish War.

The Spanish Civil War presented a difficult problem in international law and national politics. The Neutrality Act did not apply to civil conflicts, and F.D.R. could have had a free hand in the formulation of American policy toward the war. The United States had a treaty of friendship with the Loyalist Government, and Roosevelt could have aided it in a perfectly legal manner. At the same time, many Americans saw the conflict as a battle between Democracy (the Loyalists) and Fascism (the Insurgents). Roosevelt's sympathies were with the Loyalists, and he considered plans of aiding them early in 1937. Hull discussed the matter with the British and French representatives, with whom the United States hoped to cooperate. He was told that the European Democracies were committed to a hands off policy, and was urged to express this to the President. Hull agreed with the British and French, and recommended to Roosevelt that the United States follow suit.[1] The President accepted this advice and took no positive action during the war to aid the Loyalists. He did recommend a moral embargo, which passed the Senate unanimously and the House by all but one vote. The Administration and Congress expressed sympathy for the Loyalist cause, but did little else; isolationism was still in the saddle and peace came before idealism.

This view was opposed by two strikingly dissimilar groups. Many internationalists saw the war as the first battle against Fascism, and demanded that Roosevelt take a more vigorous stand. They were joined by a group of isolationists who argued for intervention on legalistic grounds as well as those of morality. Under the traditional rules of neutrality as well as the treaty with Spain, the United States had no right to withhold goods from the legitimate, recognized government. To them it would be an unneutral act to practice isolationism, since being neutral would, in effect, aid the Insurgents, who were receiving aid from Germany and Italy, and penalize the Loyalists, who had difficulty purchasing arms.[2] Isolationist historian Charles A. Beard took this position, and accepted the post of honorary chairman of the International Relief Organization. Following the same reasoning, Nye became one of the most ardent supporters of the Madrid Government.[3]

The international balance was shifting rapidly, and no one realized this more than Roosevelt. He sensed the changes, and felt that he could get more from Congress in the next neutrality act by standing aside than by actively campaigning for his program. Also, Roosevelt had made his reputation as an isolationist, and now felt that Congress would be willing to grant him a greater degree of discretion in foreign affairs than had previously been the case.

Pittman welcomed this lack of interference, and introduced a bill which he had written in January, 1937. The draft contained many of those provisions which Roosevelt had asked for and been denied in 1936. The President could embargo such non-military items as he might feel necessary and would have greater discretion in determining whether or not a state of war existed.

Realizing that such an act would destroy much of their power, Borah and Nye denounced the draft, and were joined by Vandenberg who claimed that Roosevelt would use it to ally the nation with France and Great Britain.[4] Nonetheless, the bill was well-received, and Nye had to shift to support of it in the end.[5] The bill was re-written several times, but when finally passed it gave F.D.R. more power in foreign relations than at any time since he took office. He would have to embargo shipments of arms and munitions on finding a state of war to exist, and could extend this embargo to any third nation which aided the belligerents. In cases of civil war he could also declare an embargo should he feel that the conflict would threaten or endanger the peace of the United States. Most important, F.D.R. was granted powers over the shipment of non-military items as well, and could impose conditions of cash-and-carry on munitions, thus keeping American ships out of war zones and ending the need for such artificial devices as moral embargoes.[6]

The President waited but a few months to test his new authority. With the resumption of Japanese agression in China and fears of a new war in Europe, Roosevelt felt it necessary to state the American position. On October 5 he observed that

> there is no escape through mere isolation or neutrality . . . There is a solidarity and interdependence about the modern world, both technically and morally, which makes it impossible for any nation completely to isolate itself from economic and political upheavals in the rest of the world.[7]

With this in mind, Roosevelt called upon the American people to support his plan to "quarantine the aggressors." In effect, he would apply the neutrality legislation to the attacking parties but continue to sell munitions to the victims of aggression. Roosevelt went further than public opinion of the time would accept,[8] but actually he was only returning to the position that Hoover and Stimson had held in 1932. Hull wrote that the reaction was "quick and violent" and had the effect of "setting back for at least six months our constant educational campaign intended to create and strengthen public opinion toward international cooperation."[9] Roosevelt realized this, and attempted to hedge on his statements.[10] But it was too late; the damage had been done and the disaffection of the isolationist-progressives had begun. The split deepened when F.D.R. compounded his internationalist statements with acts which demonstrated that his isolationist phase was drawing to a close. Hull's statements and actions at the Brussels Conference of 1937, when he asked for international cooperation to end the Sino-Japanese War was one aspect of this change.[11] F.D.R.'s sponsorship of the "Welles Plan" to outlaw war, limit armaments, and draw up a code of international conduct was another indication of his change of mind.[12] On May 17, 1938, he signed a bill for naval expansion, designed to create a two ocean navy.[13] The groundwork for a vigorous foreign policy was being laid. "Doctor New Deal" was ailing, and the tools for "Doctor Win-the-War" were being forged as early as 1937.

Roosevelt's new foreign policies alienated many isolationist-progressives. Republicans, New Dealers and independents who had supported him in 1932 and 1936 now left the Roosevelt camp. On November 11, 1938, Nye, Norman Thomas, Frank Kingdon and Joseph Lash joined in a strange quartet to argue for a stricter neutrality policy with less presidential discretion.[14] Realizing that unless some action was taken to stop the movement he would lose the isolationist-progressives completely, Roosevelt hinted at his willingness to replace Hull with La Follette as Secretary of State.[15] When F.D.R. was an isolationist, he had an internationalist advisor on foreign affairs. Why not an isolationist as Secretary of State now that he was again leaning toward internationalism? But the isolationist-progressives were unwilling to play under these rules. Faced with the alternative of continuing the New Deal or abandoning isolationism, F.D.R. chose the latter.[16]

This change was brought home in Roosevelt's message to Congress on January 14, 1939 when, for the first time since taking office, he asked for no important new reform legislation. Instead, he pledged the resources of his office to the cause of peace. The President reiterated his faith that the nation would be isolated from future wars, but he warned that it would be difficult to avoid taking sides in any new conflict. He offered a substitute to actual involvement. There were methods "short of war" which were "stronger and more effective than mere words" to bring home to aggressors "the aggregate sentiments of our own people."[17] One such method would be to amend the Neutrality Act so as to guarantee aid to those nations under attack. This question, along with that of the third term, dominated American politics for the rest of the year.

One result of this stand was the emergence of a new isolationist-progressive alliance which was dedicated to the continuation of reform at home and the maintenance of isolation toward Europe. This new opposition group gained strength throughout the session, and was reinforced by an alliance with anti-third term Democrats. The newspaper headlines told the story. "Congress Opens Fight to Take Back Powers," "Congressional Revolt Dominates News," "Congress Opposes Roosevelt Again" and finally, "Adjournment Ends Chapter of Presidential Defeat."[18]

Criticism of Roosevelt came from all quarters. Conservative Republicans opposed the new foreign policies as they had the rest of the Roosevelt program.[19] Now that the New Deal was drawing to a close, they could once again join with progressive Republicans. Theodore Roosevelt, Jr. warned that "we must not permit ourselves to be stampeded in our foreign policy."[20] Old New Dealers like Raymond Moley predicted that if the Roosevelt program in foreign affairs were adopted, "free criticism will be restricted . . . industries will be nationalized . . . wages and hours will be fixed . . . profits will be conscripted, and all would feel the iron hand of the Government."[21] A new group of disillusioned ex-New Dealers was created. Jerome Frank echoed Moley's predictions of future dictatorship and was followed out of the coalition by Anglophobe Democrats.[22]

Although Roosevelt's first coalition was destroyed by 1938, a new one was created out of its ashes. Many New Dealers continued to support their chief, some against their own better judgments. They were joined by eastern internationalists who rejoiced at Roosevelt's apparent rediscovery of his Wilsonian roots. Those being the days of the United Front, left wingers joined and called upon the President to link the United States with the U.S.S.R. to save the world from Fascism. A strange new member were businessmen who had opposed the President so bitterly in the past. Now that they were tasting the first fruits of pre-war European spending, they supported a program which would allow this to continue. If the isolationists had their way, said one such businessman, a new depression would hit the nation, which "could bring us to surrender our free institutions of trade and commerce to economic fascism without striking a blow in their defense." [23] Faced with new problems, new programs, and new supporters and enemies, F.D.R. delivered his first important address of 1939.

In his New Year's Message to Congress, the President placed himself squarely in the internationalist camp. He said that the neutrality acts had not served their purpose; neutrality cannot be legislated. He indicated that outright repeal should be considered, an action which would give him a free hand in dealing with the potential European War.[24] Roosevelt later added that neutrality legislation operated against the nation's best interests, and that "we might have been stronger if we did not have it." [25]

The President was a realist; he knew that outright repeal, however advantageous to the nation, hadn't a chance of passing in Congress. Together with Hull he worked out what he considered to be an acceptable compromise. Cash-and-carry would be extended and American firms would not be permitted to trade with aggressors. To placate the isolationists, Roosevelt offered to continue the arms embargo.[26] Pittman introduced the bill on March 20, but it satisfied no one; the desire to compromise was not present. Neither the isolationists nor the internationalists would settle for less than complete victory.

Failing at compromise, Roosevelt tried for everything, hoping to force the isolationists to accept his bill. "The more I think the problem through," he told Hull, "the more I am convinced that the existing Neutrality Act should be repealed in toto without any substitute."[27] The internationalists in Congress picked this up. Senator Lewis suggested that the Act be repealed and replaced by a simple declaration of neutrality, and Senator King offered a motion for repeal along with a resolution stating that the President should be entrusted with the making of foreign policy.[28] Proposals of this nature further served to unite anti-Administration forces into a solid front dedicated to preserving the Neutrality Act.[29] Senator Reynolds said that he was "sore with Britain and France because they are doing their best to lead us into another war."[30] Johnson, who by this time seemed too ill to participate in the debate, rallied for one of his many "last struggles" for his ideas.[31] Witnesses before the Senate Foreign Relations Committee averred that "William Allen White and the captains of business and finance" were trying to use the neutrality fight as a means of stirring up another war.[32] "All this Jules Verne talk about ships coming over here and bombing is all bunk" said John A. Matthews of the Paul Revere Sentinels Society. "The only bomb shelter we need in America is against the propaganda of war mongers."[33] The isolationist strength was such that the Pittman bill was defeated in committee. Roosevelt had lost the first round.

Failing to get what he wanted in the Senate, Roosevelt turned his attention to the House. Sol Bloom of New

York introduced an Administration bill to repeal the arms embargo completely. Roosevelt hoped that Bloom could rally the internationalists around him and frighten the isolationists into a spirit of compromise. This hope died when Bloom proved a bungling tactician, achieving nothing and estranging the isolationists further than before. When all seemed lost Congressman Vorys of California amended the bill to include an arms embargo and exclude mention of cash-and-carry. A sorely disappointed Roosevelt accepted the emasculated proposal, which passed the House by a vote of 201-187.[34]

The Senate isolationists were stronger than those in the House. Johnson and Borah were willing to accept the amended Bloom Bill, which they felt marked a return of power to the Congress.[35] On the other hand, Nye and Clark, feeling that Roosevelt had now unmasked himself as a Wilsonian, refused to accept any compromise. Since they were not sure that they could muster enough votes to stop the bill before the Senate, they concentrated their attack in the more limited confines of the Foreign Relations Committee. Aided by Democrats Guy Gillette of Iowa and George of Georgia the Republican minority was able to block consideration of the bill by a vote of 12-11.[35]

The Administration was stunned by this unexpected action. Roosevelt accused the Committee of playing into the hands of the European dictators and asked Attorney General Murphy how he could best circumvent Congress in the determination of foreign policy.[36] The cash-and-carry provisions had already lapsed and, in the absence of new legislation, the United States could take no action to aid the European Democracies. A new bill would not be considered until Congress met in January of 1940. Hull shared F.D.R.'s concern. "What might not happen before then! In those six months the fate of the civilized world might be at stake." [37] Together they planned a new means of approaching the isolationists. Hull drew up a program which would limit the President as to specific actions but would grant him leeway in the broader interpretations of the law.[38] This plan was presented to Republican leaders at a White House conference on July 18. Roosevelt, Hull, Barkley, Garner and Pittman represented the Democrats while Borah, Austin and McNary spoke for the Republicans. The President began by attempting to split the isolationist coalition. He suggested that he and Borah could agree on moderate proposals, while Nye was unalterably against compromise. Perhaps a union of the two on foreign policy could be forged. Borah refused to bite, insisting that the Administration miscalculated the need for discretionary legislation. When he intimated that his sources of information in coming to this conclusion were better than those of the State Department, Hull exploded.[39] F.D.R. tried to smooth the differences, but Borah wouldn't budge. Finally Garner turned to Roosevelt and remarked, "Well, Captain, we might as well face the facts. You haven't the votes and that's all there is to it." [40] Roosevelt admitted defeat, but did not quit the battle. During his August 8 press conference he charged that Congress had "bet the Nation, made a large wager with the Nation, which may effect, if they lose it, about a billion and a half human beings."

> They have said, "There will be no war until sufficiently long after we come back in January so that we can take care of things after we come back," and I sincerely hope

> they are right. But, if they are not right and we have another serious international crisis they have tied my hands, and I have practically no power to make an American effort to prevent such a war from breaking out. Now, that is a pretty serious responsibility.[41]

With the outbreak of war in September, Roosevelt had to face this problem. He took to the radio a few hours after the French and British declarations of war, promising that "as long as it remains within my power to prevent, there will be no blackout of peace in the United States." F.D.R. significantly added that he could not ask every American "to remain neutral in thought as well." [42]

The war all but ended the great debate between internationalists and isolationists. Roosevelt's speech indicated that the United States could no longer pretend that Europe did not exist and that war could not affect the Western Hemisphere. The isolationists themselves realized this, and began to adopt the label of "non-interventionist." The isolationist was uninterested in what happened overseas, and would concentrate instead on the American continent. The non-interventionist also considered the nation to be unique, and would remain as aloof from foreign affairs as possible. He would oppose all attempts to draw the United States into foreign wars, but at the same time he would educate himself as to what the issues were, and would be willing to take *positive actions* to insulate the nation against these wars. The non-interventionists included in their numbers such diverse figures as Herbert Hoover, William Randolph Hearst, General Van Horn Mosely, Father Coughlin, Norman Thomas, the German-American Bund and World Peaceways.[43] The Keep America Out of War Committee brought together Bruce Bliven of the *New Republic,* Morris Ernst, Frank Graham, Nye and Clark. Harry Emerson Fosdick joined with Burt Wheeler in agreeing that the United States must not become involved in the war.[44]

These strange partnerships were the result of the general dislocation which took place when international affairs intruded on the New Deal. When this happened the reformer found himself faced with a dilemma. Should he follow F.D.R., one of the most reform-minded presidents in history, or should he turn to those who claimed that Roosevelt had betrayed reform when he chose to exert American power overseas? Should he follow Norman Thomas, who argued for non-intervention, or William Allen White, who said that "the European democracies are carrying our banner" and that "the democracies west of the Rhine and north of the Baltic are digging our front line trenches"?[45] Interventionists like White were not internationalists. Indeed, most of them were isolationists in the twenties and early thirties. They argued that the first duty of the nation was self-preservation, and that in the context of international affairs in 1939 this meant intervening temporarily in European affairs. When the crisis ended, the United States should withdraw. The American mission was confined to this nation, and we had neither the right nor the duty to spread it elsewhere. The internationalism of Woodrow Wilson was almost dead by 1939; Hull was little more than a fossil of a period when Americans thought they were fighting for the world as well as themselves. By 1939 most Americans were isolationists. Those who felt that they could practice this doctrine during wartime took the non-interventionist position, while those who were willing to modify the doctrine for a period of time became interventionists. The question was whether the preservation of American neutrality and domestic reform was more or less important than preventing the dictators from taking over the rest of the world. The interventionist and non-interventionist differed as to degree, while the isolationist and internationalist were diametrically opposed. Thus, by late 1939 there was more of a consensus in American foreign policy attitudes than two or three years before. In addition, the pre-war battles between liberals and conservatives, reformers and reactionaries, dissolved into the new struggle of interventionist vs. non-interventionist. This is still the case today.

Borah stated the non-interventionist case to the American people in a radio address on September 14, during which he tacitly admitted that isolationism was impossible and that the American public could not but desire an Allied victory. He noted, however, that wars undermine freedom, and pleaded for a careful consideration of the consequences before allowing the President to take actions which might lead to American involvement. "It is not hatred of another country," said Borah, "but love of our own which makes for wisdom and justice in the formation of national policies." [46] The Senator struck a responsive chord. He received over 100,000 letters in regard to his talk, most of which favored non-interventionism.[47] Roosevelt responded by quietly organizing the Senate in favor of repeal of the arms embargo, a move which would permit him to send munitions to the Allies.[48] Borah and Roosevelt became the poles around which non-interventionists and interventionists rallied.[49] During the special session of Congress called to frame American policy toward the war, it was evident that Borah and his friends were in the minority.

The interventionist mood could best be seen in the nature of those former isolationists who joined F.D.R.'s campaign to repeal the arms embargo. Senator Norris supported Roosevelt's stand and Al Smith, formerly Roosevelt's most severe Democratic critic, backed him because "he is so obviously right." [50] Senators Glass and Byrd, leaders of the Party's conservative wing, announced their support, as did Burke of Nebraska, Byrnes and Smith of South Carolina and Bailey of North Carolina. Even Pat Harrison, who had been deposed as Senate Majority Leader, and George, whose distrust of Roosevelt had been evident since 1936, climbed on the bandwagon.[51] During the first days of the special session the National Republican Club went on record in favor of aid to the Allies.[52] By the middle of September, Roosevelt could have repealed the arms embargo with little difficulty. Non-interventionists were either silent or joined with Roosevelt on this issue. Senator Thomas observed that "if neutrality means a crushing of world morality, it is better to take sides and fight." [53] Freshman Senator Robert Taft favored repeal, seeing nothing unneutral in "the shipment of munitions of war to any nation who comes and gets them." [54] Taft claimed that opening American factories to belligerents was not a violations of neutrality, and that cash-and-carry was "a most important step toward keeping this country out of war." [55] "More than this we are not prepared to do," editorialized the *New Republic*, "but less than this is too little." [56]

Realizing that Congress was behind him in desiring to end the arms embargo, Roosevelt decided to shoot for complete repeal of the Neutrality Act. Hull warned F.D.R. that he was making the same mistake as he did in delivering the quarantine speech two years before. By running too far in advance of public opinion he could lose those gains he already had made. Pittman warned that he would be lucky to get five votes for such a program in the Foreign Relations Committee, and McNary added that "the trouble is that people would think, if we repealed the whole Neutrality Act, that we were repealing our neutrality." Nevertheless, F.D.R. was intent on such a course of action. On September 21, he addressed the special session.

> I seek a greater consistency through the repeal of the embargo provisions, and a return to international law. I seek reenactment of the historic and traditional American policy which, except for the disastrous interlude of the Embargo and Non-Intercourse Acts, has served us well from the very beginning of our Constitutional existence.

This historic message served to destroy the consensus of opinion which existed on repeal of the arms embargo. As Hull and Pittman had predicted, a non-interventionist coalition appeared overnight. Pittman was its first victim. His unwillingness to lead the Roosevelt program meant that F.D.R. had to select a new Administration foreign policy spokesman. James Byrnes was approached and offered the position, which he accepted on condition that he be given a free hand in regard to tactics.[57] This was accepted, and he skilfully obtained commitments from many congressmen and senators for the Administration program.[58] Hull was the pen of the Administration and Byrnes its voice for the next few weeks. Together they steered a new bill—which included repeal of the arms embargo and the re-introduction of cash-and-carry-through the Foreign Relations Committee by a vote of 16-7.[59]

The Senate debate saw the non-interventionists using all of their heavy artillery in an attempt to batter down the Administration bill. "It is not our war," said Borah, and Walsh observed that "if embargo repeal is neutrality, God save America." Nye charged that "the people are being led, driven, teased, and cajoled into war." Holt predicted that the plan would "send the country down the path of involvement."[60] Few interventionists bothered to answer these charges. Byrnes and Roosevelt instructed them to shut off debate and get the bill passed as soon as possible.[61] The strategy was sound. After an attempt by Clark to amend the bill failed, it passed the Senate by a vote of 63-30.[62]

Roosevelt expected the margin of victory in the House to be closer than this. Farley reported that conservative Democrats thought cash-and-carry was too "radical" and their votes might bring the measure to defeat.[63] Ickes predicted victory by twenty votes and Garner by forty as Sam Rayburn was called in to whip the Democrats into line behind the bill. F.D.R. personally called many congressmen and asked for their aid.[64] They did their work well; on November 2, the House passed the bill by a vote of 243-181.[65]

Roosevelt then called a meeting of key members of both houses to hammer out differences between the House and Senate versions, and on November 3 the Neutrality Act of 1939—a curiously named piece of legislation considering its content—passed the Senate by a vote of 55-24 and the House by 243-172.[66] F.D.R. signed the bill on the following day, thus ending a chapter in the history of American neutrality.

The Administration was jubilant.[67] It had attained the much desired freedom to aid the Allies; interventionism had been given its first mandate. Despite this victory, the bill was essentially moderate. Roosevelt did not have the powers to grant credits or loans to the Allies and the cash-and-carry provision forfeited some of our freedom of the seas. Since foreign nations were expected to send their merchantmen to the United States to transport arms, American shippers stood to lose a fortune in carrying charges. They rushed to transfer the registry of their vessels in order to circumvent the law, but the Maritime Commission blocked these actions as soon as they were initiated, and Roosevelt stated that such manipulations would not be tolerated.[68]

The bill did allow the Allies to step up their purchases of American goods. Roosevelt's application of the Neutrality Act at the beginning of war had forced Great Britain and France to cancel more than $78 million worth of orders.[69] Now some $72 million was earmarked for the purchase of planes and ammunition alone.[70] The United States was becoming the arsenal of democracy.

Despite this, non-interventionism remained potent. Its appeals found a ready audience among those Americans who feared that the nation would again be drawn into a war which was none of their concern. The non-interventionists admitted sympathy for the Allies, but on the other hand would not admit that they were much better morally than the Axis. Chamberlain and Daladier did not capture the American imagination in 1939 as did Churchill and De Gaulle in 1940. The non-interventionist's use of moral arguments was a key weakness. What would they do should a completely "good" European state be attacked by a nation that most Americans considered the personification of evil? The non-interventionists did not consider this problem in November, but within a month they were forced to deal with it when the Russo-Finnish War began.

NOTES

Chapter III: THE GREAT DEBATE AND THE EMERGENCE OF INTERVENTIONISM

1 *New York Tribune,* November 19, 1939; Hull, *Memoirs,* I, 476-78; *Peace and War, 1931-1941,* pp. 322-23.

2 *New York Tribune,* January 7, 1937. For a detailed monograph on this subject, see F. Jay Taylor, *The United States and the Spanish Civil War, 1936-1939* (New York, 1958).

3 Hull, *Memoirs,* I, 510-11.

4 *New York Times,* January 24, March 3, 25, 1937; Edwin Borchard and William P. Lage, *Neutrality for the United States* (New Haven, 1940), p. 328.

5 Hull, *Memoirs,* I, 510-11.

6 *Peace and War, 1931-1941,* pp. 355-65.

7 *New York Times,* October 6, 1937.

8 William L. Langer and S. Everett Gleason, *The Challenge to Isolation, 1937-1940* (New York, 1952), pp. 19-20.

9 Hull, *Memoirs,* I, 545.

10 The hedging was evident in F.D.R.'s press conference of October 6, 1938. See *The Public Papers of Franklin D. Roosevelt,* VI, 423-25.

11 Hull, *Memoirs,* I, 550-56.

12 Langer and Gleason, *Challenge to Isolation,* pp. 20-22.

13 Rauch, *Roosevelt From Munich to Pearl Harbor,* p. 60; *New York Tribune,* May 18, 1938.

14 Leaflet on deposit at New York Public Library.

15 Ickes, *Secret Diary,* II, 395.

16 John Gunther, *Roosevelt in Retrospect* (New York, 1950), p. 300; Eric F. Goldman, *Rendezvous With Destiny* (New York, 1952), pp. 374-75.

17 Hull, *Memoirs,* I, 612.

18 *New York Times,* January 15, July 2, August 13, 1939; *Scholastic* (Vol. 35, No. 9, September 18, 1939), p. 12.

19 Quincy Howe, *Blood Is Cheaper Than Water* (New York, 1939), pp. 24-25.

20 *Vital Speeches* (Vol. 5, No. 20, August 1, 1939), pp. 618-20.

21 Moley, *After Seven Years,* p. 384

22 Jerome Frank, *Save America First* (New York, 1938), pp. 156-57.

23 James Cromwell, *Isolation vs. Democracy* (Newark, 1939), pp. 6-8.

24 *Public Papers of Franklin D. Roosevelt,* VIII, 12.

25 *Ibid.,* VIII, 155; Hull, *Memoirs,* I, 641.

26 Hull, *Memoirs,* I, 613-14.

27 *Ibid.,* I, 641.

28 Francis O. Wilcox,"The Neutrality Fight in Congress: 1939" (*The American Political Science Review,* Vol. 33, No. 5, October, 1939), pp. 811-12.

29 *Nation* (Vol. 148, March 18, 1939), pp. 307-8.

30 United States Senate, Committee on Foreign Relations, 76th Congress, 1st Session, *Hearings Before the Committee on Foreign Relations,* Part 1 (Washington, 1939), p. 29.

31 *Ibid.,* p. 17; Ickes, *Secret Diary,* II, 139.

32 *Foreign Relations Committee Hearings,* pp. 432-40.

33 *Ibid.,* p. 433.

34 Joseph Alsop and Robert Kintner, *American White Paper* (New York, 1940), p. 42; Wilcox, *Neutrality Fight in Congress,* p. 814; *Congressional Record,* June 29, 1939, p. 8304 ff.; Hull, *Memoirs,* I, 646.

35 *New York Times,* July 9, 25, 1939; *Newsweek* (Vol. 14, No. 4, July 24, 1939), p. 15.

36 *New Republic* (Vol. 99, No. 1287, August 2, 1939), p. 361; *F.D.R.: His Personal Letters,* III, 899-900.

37 Hull, *Memoirs,* I, 648.

38 *Ibid.,* I, 645; *Public Papers of Franklin D. Roosevelt,* VIII, 380-81; *Peace and War, 1931-4941,* p. 473.

39 Hull, *Memoirs,* I, 649-50; *Newsweek* (Vol. 14, No. 5, July 31, 1939), p. 5.

40 Alsop and Kintner, *American White Paper,* p. 46.

41 *Public Papers of Franklin D. Roosevelt,* VIII, 428-29.

42 *Ibid.,* VIII, 460-64.

43 John Crosby Brown, "American Isolationism" (*Foreign Affairs,* Vol. 18, No. 1, October, 1939), p. 31.

44 George V. Denny, Jr., "What's Your Opinion?" (*Current History,* Vol. 51, No. 2, October, 1939), pp. 42-46. Max Lerner and Quincy Howe, both prominent internationalists in previous battles, were also members of this Committee.

45 Johnson, *Battle Against Isolationism,* pp. 47-48.

46 *New York Times,* September 15, 1939.

47 *Newsweek* (Vol. 14, No. 13, September 25, 1939), p. 7.

48 Ickes, *Secret Diary,* III, 7-8.

49 For public opinion of the time, and evidence that polarization had begun, see Cantril, *Public Opinion,* p. 678.

50 *New York Times,* October 2, 3, 1939; *Christian Science Monitor,* September 20, 1939.

51 Johnson, *Battle Against Isolationism,* p. 15 ff.; *New York Times,* October 1, 1939.

52 *New York Times,* October 2, 1939.

53 (Washington) *Evening Star,* September 11, 1939.

54 *Congressional Digest* (Vol. 18, No. 10, October, 1939), p. 245.

55 *New York Times,* October 13, 1939.

56 "America's Role in the War" (*New Republic,* Vol. 100, No. 1292, September 6, 1939), pp. 116-17.

57 Alsop and Kintner, *American White Paper,* pp. 73-75; *Public Papers of Franklin D. Roosevelt,* VIII, 512-22; Byrnes, *All in One Lifetime,* 110-14. Roosevelt and Pittman never got along well together, and F.D.R. welcomed this opportunity to dump what he considered dead weight. See "The Morgenthau Diaries, Part III" (*Collier's,* Vol. 120, No. 15, October 11, 1947), p. 79 and *F.D.R.: His Personal Letters,* II, 934.

58 James Byrnes, *Speaking Frankly* (New York, 1947), pp. 7-8.

59 One newspaper article read: "Although Majority Leader Barkley and Chairman Pittman of the Foreign Relations Committee are the nominal leaders in the fight for repeal, the 60 year old South Carolina Democrat, slight, nervous, and dynamic, will be the actual field marshal of the Administration's forces." *New York Post,* September 25, 1939; Hull, *Memoirs,* I, 695; *Roosevelt Papers* in Langer and Gleason, *Challenge to Isolation,* p. 225.

60 *Congressional Record,* 76th Congress, 2nd Session, Vol. 85, Part I, pp. 45-48.

61 *F.D.R.: His Personal Letters,* III, 924; *Newsweek* (Vol. 14, No. 16, October 16, 1939), p. 30.

62 *New York Times,* October 28, 1939; Hull, *Memoirs,* I, 695-97.

63 Ickes, *Secret Diary,* III, 43.

64 *Ibid.,* III, 38, 51; *New York Daily News,* November 1, 1939; *F.D.R.: His Personal Letters,* III, 946.

65 *New York Times,* November 3, 1939.

66 *Christian Science Monitor,* November 3, 1939; *New York Times,* November 4, 1939.

67 Johnson, *Battle Against Isolationism,* p. 53.

68 *Christian Science Monitor,* November 6, 1939.

69 *New York Post,* October 25, 1939.

70 *Wall Street Journal,* November 24, 1939; *Newsweek* (Vol. 14, No. 20, November 13, 1939), p. 15.

Chapter IV

THE WINTER WAR BEGINS

Americans knew very little about Finland prior to World War II. In 1919 the nation applauded when the Finns broke away from Russia and a small American relief mission was sent to the embryonic republic. At the Paris Olympic Games of 1925 the name of Paavo Nurmi became identified with track prowess, and sports-minded Americans showed some interest in the country of his birth. Music lovers knew Finland through Jan Sibelius, whose compositions were popular in the United States. While other European nations defaulted on their debts, Finland paid hers with regularity, and this fact was not overlooked when the newspapers castigated Great Britain and France. If proud little Finland can pay, why can't the great western democracies? While the Volstead Act was changing American morals, some few might have noted that Finland was also experimenting with prohibition, meeting with as little success as the United States.[1] Otherwise, the man in the street knew as much about Finland as he did of Mongolia. One American who joined the Finnish Army in 1939, wrote that prior to that time all he knew of Finland was that "it was somewhere up around the North Pole and that Finland had paid her war debts."[2]

Actually, there was no good reason why the American people—who knew little enough about larger and more important nations—*should* know more about Finland. Those Finns who had migrated to the United States did not advertise or propagandize for their homeland as did the more numerous Irish, Germans and Italians.[3] Nor did they introduce striking new customs or innovations to the American scene, or keep their culture intact as did the Jews. Most of them left Finland as a result of prolonged economic depressions or to escape military service. Religious and political pressures were lacking for the most part and the educated, urban classes which usually provide leadership for newly-arrived immigrant groups remained at home.[4]

The keystone of Finnish-American relations was the payment of the war debt which, interestingly enough, had been incurred *after* the war had ended. The total indebtedness was $9 million plus interest to 1984, when payments were to be completed. Annual remittances fluctuated, the largest to be $356,185 in 1933. A cheap price to pay for American friendship! In that year the State Department offered to reduce payments in view of the world economic crisis. Finland insisted on paying in full, thus reaping a harvest of favorable publicity.[5] There was one honest European nation, said the press, and that was Finland. The actual sum was rarely mentioned, and the fact that the amount was so small that Finland, unlike France and Great Britain, could pay without deranging her finances, was usually overlooked.[6]

In sharp contrast to these favorable sentiments toward Finland were the strong negative feelings held by most Americans toward the Soviet Union. The Communist regime seemed a revolutionary dictatorship which was anti-capitalist, anti-religious, and opposed to all of the social and moral values cherished by the American people. The Bolshevist, with his black beard, fierce expression and incendiary actions was etched into the American imagination. During the twenties and early thirties reports from the U.S.S.R. were scattered and highly opinionated. The vast majority of the press had strong anti-Soviet biases. Only a relatively few social reformers and, of course, the Communists, would defend the actions of the U.S.S.R. during the interbellum period.[7] Almost every report from there "struck a metallic prejudice composed of America's attitude toward domestic problems, foreign affairs, religious differences, political traditions, etc." [8] In this period the only sources of opinion which were free from this bias were the small "liberal weeklies." [9]

The course of Soviet-American relations is not within the scope of this work. Official relations, however, can only be characterized as stormy. The United States did not recognize the Soviet Government until 1933. In return for recognition the Soviets promised not to interfere in American internal affairs, agreed to discuss existing claims, and to maintain the most favored nation principle in trade. All of these promises were broken, and relations became progressively worse.[10]

By the last months of 1938 the American Government realized that however the nation felt about the Soviet Union, her armed strength dictated better relations with the Communist leaders. The western democracies were trying to improve relations with Stalin and repair the damage caused by the snubbing of the Soviet leader at Munich. As early as August, Roosevelt tried to use his influence in bringing the Soviets into an agreement with France and Great Britain. Hull initiated conversations with Soviet Ambassador Troyanovsky and it was hoped that from these talks an alliance against Hitler could be formed.[11] Needless to say, these attempts failed. After the Nazi-Soviet Pact, American opinion was more anti-Soviet than before. The war in Europe, if and when it came, would now be simplified for the American people. "The sham fronts are down, and the anti-democratic system are on one side and the democracies on the other." [12]

The Nazi-Soviet Pact also marked the beginning of a new wave of left-wing disillusionment with the Soviet Union. Many members of the Communist Party and its satellite organizations defected as the essentially anti-liberal biases of their leaders became more evident. Communist officials had a difficult time explaining the Nazi alliance and the sudden shift in Soviet foreign policy. Earl Browder, who at one time stated that there was more likelihood of him being elected to the American Chamber of Commerce than of Germany and the U.S.S.R. signing such a treaty, was forced to backtrack. He now claimed that the pact had, in effect, limited the aggressions of Fascism by turning Germany away from the Soviet Union. *The New Masses* called it "a burglary insurance policy which Soviet diplomacy has been forced to take out against the threat of another and more dangerous Munich." [13]

The Soviet occupation of Poland caused American indignation to rise to still greater heights. The man in the street now considered Hitler and Stalin full-fledged partners. "This is a nightmare," wrote one official. "It recalls Genghis Khan." [14] The American Government did all that was possible under the circumstances to aid the Polish exiles, and offered President Moscicki a refuge in the United States.[15] The exiles were recognized as the legitimate representatives of Poland, and Washington established diplomatic relations with the Government in Exile on October 2.[16]

While sympathizing with the Poles, Roosevelt and Hull refrained from taking any action which might place the U.S.S.R. on the same plane as the Axis powers. The Neutrality Act was not extended to the Soviets, although the attack on Poland would seem to have justified such a course of action. Hull feared that such a move would "thrust her further into Hitler's arms." "We had the feeling that Russia and Germany would not become full allies," he later wrote, "and that Hitler had not abandoned his ambition with regard to Russia."[17] The difficulties of such a stand were evident. On the one hand Hull had to make it part of the record that the United States deplored the rape of Poland, while on the other the U.S.S.R. had to be kept out of the Axis partnership at all costs. The Secretary hoped that by acting cautiously the United States could be the agent which would lead Stalin into the anti-Fascist coalition.

This was the situation when the U.S.S.R. began making threatening gestures toward Finland in the fall of 1939. To most Americans it seemed as though Stalin was determined to gobble up as much territory as he could while Hitler was busy on the western front. Actually, in the secret protocols to the Nazi-Soviet Pact, Germany had ceded Finland to the U.S.S.R. as a sphere of influence.[18] Indeed, prior to the negotiations Moscow had notified Berlin that were the independence of Finland threatened, the Red Army would march to the northern frontier.[19] Hitler was willing to sacrifice the Baltic to Stalin in return for full acceptance of his plans for

Poland, and it was on this basis that the Nazi-Soviet Pact was signed.[20]

Poland was occupied in September as per agreement, and in October Stalin "pacified" Latvia, Lithuania and Estonia while Hitler stood aside.[21] At the same time negotiations were initiated between Finland and the U.S.S.R.

The Soviet demands on Finland were not as great as the West had expected. In return for land in the south of Finland, Stalin offered a larger amount of territory in the north of the Soviet Union.[22] This trade would enable the U.S.S.R. to gain strategic control of the Baltic Sea while Finland would be reimbursed with some of the best timberland in the Soviet Union. The Soviets did not present this plan in the form of an ultimatum, as had been the case with the Baltic States. Formal negotiations began in Moscow on October 5 and lasted almost three months, during which time Stalin backed down on several important points.[23] He remained unmovable on one condition, however: Finland must cede the southern approaches to Leningrad to the Soviet Union.[24] When the Finnish emissaries refused to consider this, negotiations were discontinued. For a few weeks Finland rejoiced, believing that the U.S.S.R. would not press the matter further. Toward the middle of December Stalin demonstrated that the last words remained to be spoken. He accused Finland of having designs on Soviet territories, and prepared for a "Finnish attack." On December 29 the Red Army advanced into Finland in what the Soviet press called "a war of defense."[25]

American diplomats were not surprised by this development. The State Department had known of the

Soviet desire for Finnish bases as early as April of 1939, and from the first had tried to aid the Finns.[26] True to Hull's policies, however, no action was taken which might have served to alienate the Soviets.[27] This was brought home to the Finns as early as the summer of 1939, when a Finnish request for a loan to construct a northern railroad was evaded by American officials.[28] In October another loan application was made, this time for $50 million. Although the money was for non-military purposes, Hull refused to consider the loan which he feared would be used to build up the Finnish Army.[29] During the next month applications for loans were shunted back and forth by Treasury Secretary Morgenthau and R.F.C. chief Jesse Jones. Eventually the hot potato was juggled back to Hull's offices, where A. A. Berle, Jr. took the matter under consideration. The Finns were notified that should they desire export licenses for arms and munitions, "prompt consideration will be given." [30] The request for credits, however, was buried.

Despite this rebuff Finnish Ambassador Hjalmar Procope continued to press for American aid. A young, handsome and gregarious diplomat, he obviously liked the United States and its institutions and eventually married an American. "His personality has within a few months swept Washington," wrote one columnist, who called Procope a "warm friend of Mr. Roosevelt." [31] His Soviet opposite number, Constantine Oumansky, was disliked as much as Procope was liked. When news of his appointment was received, F.D.R. jokingly gave orders to double the White House guards.[32] Hull wrote that Oumansky was one of the most difficult ambassadors with whom he had to deal, a man who did much harm to Soviet-

American relations.[33] But personalities must be forgotten in diplomacy; despite these attributes of Procope and Oumansky, the Finns were given little reason to expect American aid during the negotiations. When Procope asked Hull to indicate the American position toward the Moscow talks to Oumansky, the Secretary refused, saying that such an action "would not be within the function of our Government." Just before the Soviet attack Hull told Procope that regardless of the long Finnish-American friendship and his own personal liking for the young diplomat, the United States would under no circumstances project itself "into political controversies between two other countries." He added that considering the precarious condition of Soviet-American relations at the time, an American appeal to the Soviets would probably do more harm than good.[34]

Soviet-American relations reached a low point around this time. On October 9 the steamer *City of Flint*, under American registry, was captured by the German pocket battleship *Deutschland* as it left a British harbor. The Germans put a prize crew aboard and took the vessel to the Norwegian port of Tromso. Oslo ruled that German retention of the American crew was contrary to the provisions of the Hague Neutrality Convention and requested their release. When the Germans refused, the ship was ordered to leave the harbor. Since the British blockade of the North Sea prevented the Germans from taking the ship to one of their own ports, the *Deutschland's* captain ordered the crew to proceed to Murmansk.

Washington's attempts to obtain information as to the status of the vessel and its crew met with Soviet indifference. After a week marked by growing American impatience with Soviet methods and a flurry of cablegrams from Hull to the Soviet Foreign Office, the *City of Flint* left Murmansk with a German crew in command. Stalin's refusal to antagonize his German partner enraged most Americans. Eventually the ship put in at a Norwegian port and Oslo turned its command back to the Americans, just as American newspapers began to call for some "action against the U.S.S.R. stronger than cablegrams." [35]

By the end of October the Administration found itself in a difficult position. The Finns were never more popular or the Soviets less. A show of friendship in the form of a loan to Finland would have been applauded, but at the same time might force Stalin closer to the Axis camp. In addition, the Neutrality Act was then under discussion and such a move might have caused some of the more moderate Senate isolationists to oppose the President on this important legislation. As a politician, F.D.R. had no way of knowing how such a course of action would affect the Democratic Party's chances in the elections. The problem was by no means the most crucial of F.D.R.'s career, but there were few more delicate.[36]

Sensing this difficulty and attempting to influence American actions, Finnish Premier Cajander delivered a speech on October 9 which was devoted to Finnish-Soviet relations, and the American role in the Moscow talks. Cajander expressed the hope that "Americans will watch our coming negotiations closely." [37] Swedish Ambassador Bostrom called on Hull soon after and asked for Amer-assistance for Finland, but Hull again refused.[38] Prince Gustav Adolf of Sweden then instructed Bostrom to bypass Hull and present his personal appeal to F.D.R., which the Ambassador did. Since Hull was absent from Washington at the time, the President saw Bostrom alone. Roosevelt agreed to send an appeal to President Kalinin of the U.S.S.R. expressing American concern for Finland. Hull was furious when he learned of this, and succeeded in toning down Roosevelt's strong draft message. While this was going on the Norwegian Ambassador was asked by the press whether the United States, Sweden and Norway were planning to intervene in Moscow for Finland. His refusal to comment on this caused rumors of direct American intervention to be circulated.[39] Hull informed Roosevelt of this development, and warned the President that should he take any action he would set a dangerous precedent as well as worsen the already deteriorating Soviet-American relations. Roosevelt agreed with the Secretary, and his message to Kalinin merely expressed "the earnest hope that the Soviet Union will make no demands on Finland which are inconsistent with the maintenance and development of amicable and peaceful relations between the two countries and the independence of each."[40] Kalinin replied in a polite note which evaded the issue and intimated that the United States had no business interfering in the Moscow discussions.[41] Foreign Commissar Molotov was not as polite. In a speech before the Supreme Soviet on October 30 he denounced the United States in harsh terms, warning against meddling in the talks. He suggested that Washington attend to its own business. "The Philippines and Cuba (*sic.*) . . . have for a long time demanded liberty and freedom from the United States without being able to obtain it." American attempts to interfere in European problems would only serve to "intensify, aggravate and protract them."[42] The speech was well publicized in the United States and sparked a new wave of anti-Soviet sentiment.[43]

The friction thus generated aided F.D.R. in his fight against the Neutrality Act. Americans seemed more willing than before to take an interest in foreign affairs, and this feeling was reflected in Congress.[44] Roosevelt was given the tools he demanded, but he seemed loath to use them in the Soviet-Finnish situation. No one seemed to know what he would do should the Moscow talks break down.[45]

In contrast to official vacillation and apparent indecision, the press was decidedly pro-Finnish. Interventionists and non-interventionists alike showed a marked disposition to take sides. A similar reaction took place when Poland was attacked, but pro-Finnish sentiments were greater than those for the Poles. One newspaper editorialized that a Soviet attack on Finland "would cause a wave of resentment greater even than was the case when Poland was overrun."[46] The Soviets were called "brutes," "savages," and "despoilers," while the Finns were applauded as "the defenders of western civilization" and "heroic bastions against Asiatic Communism."[47] Despite this bombast, the editors could offer little hope of American action. Finland would have to "give up a few port rights or naval bases if necessary" in order to preserve its independence.[48] Should war break out the powerful Red Army would destroy that state, and the United States would have no recourse but to stand aside and express sympathy for Finland. If Washington vacillated between indecision and homilies, the press played the role of a barking dog with no teeth.

The Moscow talks were reported in much the same fashion as a boxing match. There were few reporters who demonstrated a real understanding of the Finnish position in 1939. Americans were urged to take sides in a contest which all hoped would never take place. By the beginning of December these sentiments had jelled, led by an irresponsible press which entered the vacuum left by official indecision.

This was the situation as war approached in the North. On November 28, Hull received a telegram from Ambassador Bullitt in Paris, informing him that the U.S.S.R. had denounced her non-aggression pact with Finland and soon would attack. Roosevelt immediately cabled the American Embassy in Helsinki for further information, as Procope pleaded for an American offer of good offices to prevent the imminent war.[49] Roosevelt agreed, and a message of this nature was sent to Helsinki and Moscow the next day.[50] The offer was a futile gesture. Finland accepted with alacrity, while the Soviets refused to consider the proposition. "All we are doing," said one American official, "is making the record." [51]

The attack on Finland did not come as a surprise, but it did throw many public officials in Europe and the United States into a state of near panic. What would this mean for the Allied-Axis War? In Great Britain some called for a united front with Finland against the Soviet and Nazi dictators.[52] Italians demanded that Rome join in an anti-Soviet War.[53] From his death-bed, old Kaiser Wilhelm called for a war which would pit all of western Europe—including Germany and Great Britain—against the "Eastern Menace of International Communism." [54] When these cries died down, Europe settled down once again to waiting out the "phony war." The Soviet-Finnish conflict had little effect on this struggle.

The United States, which was not involved in war, could afford to demonstrate its pro-Finnish enthusiasm longer and louder than the Europeans. The position of Finland in 1939 seemed similar to that of Belgium in 1914. Once again a small state was being attacked by a larger one, and once again American sympathies were extended to the victim of aggression. Nowhere were the Finns supported with more gusto than in the United States; never had Finland's reputation been so high or the U.S.S.R.'s so low. "At no time in their history—not even in the grim aftermath of the First World War—had Russia and America confronted each other with greater antagonism" wrote one newspaper, while another editorialized that "another Spartan band was standing firm at Thermopylae and battling single handed not only for itself but for all of Western civilization." [55] Americans were almost unanimous in their support of Finland. Some had defended Hitler's position when he attacked Poland, but now only Communists and fellow-travellers sought to explain away the Soviet aggressions. The press used such phrases as "ruthless savagery . . . murderous and unprovoked attack . . . sheer brutality of the Soviet Union . . . peculiarly revolting lust of Stalin . . . completely unjustifiable attack." [56] The more influential columnists reflected the same sentiments. Interventionists like Dorothy Thompson and Walter Winchell filled their articles with anti-Soviet statements, the former calling Stalin uncivilized while Winchell praised Finland as a "land of heroes." [57] Non-interventionist George Sokolsky characterized the Soviet Government as being "bloody since its inception," while Col. Robert McCormick wrote that the aggressors would "feel the full moral indignation of the entire civilized world for their infamous deeds." [58] Walter Lippman called for "diplomatic support for Finland and practical measures now to stop the advance of Soviet Russia." "It is more dangerous to abandon the Finns than to help them," he wrote, and his words seemed to echo the thoughts of the majority of the members of his profession.[59] Many public figures joined in the condemnation of the U.S.S.R. and the praise of Finland. Fiorello LaGuardia said that "democracy is on the side of Finland, civilization is on the side of Finland, and Finland is on the side of God." Herbert Hoover called the Red Army "butchers" and the cautious Hull, placed in a difficult position, went so far as to say that he was "deeply shocked." [60] Harold Ickes reflected the popular sentiment when he wrote of the war in his diary on December 3.

> Russia has invaded Finland and that brave little country is standing up manfully against overwhelming forces. . . . I do not know of anything that Russia could have done that would more surely affect public opinion in this country adversely. I believe that there is a feeling of hardly suppressed rage over here that this fine and upstanding little country, with its civilization of a high order, should be ruthlessly assaulted by the Russian barbarians. Stalin is more than out-Hitlering Hitler. . . . He (is) . . . a ruthless and brutal man, and what he is doing now fully confirms this feeling.[61]

Thus, Americans had a deep emotional and moral commitment in the Soviet-Finnish conflict. Could the non-interventionists be effective in this charged atmosphere? The London *Times* thought not, and rejoiced in the American reaction. The Winter War, it said, marked "an important step toward United States intervention . . . in the establishment of governmental morality in the world."[62]

NOTES

Chapter IV: THE WINTER WAR BEGINS

1 John A. Wourinen, *The Prohibition Experiment in Finland* (New York, 1931).

2 Robert A. Winston, *Aces Wild* (New York, 1941), p. 13.

3 John Wargelin, "The Finnish-Americans" in Francis J. Brown and Joseph S. Roucek, eds., *Our Racial and National Minorities* (New York, 1937), p. 286; American Guide Series, *The Swedes and Finns in New Jersey* (New York, 1930), p. 20 ff.

4 Wargelin, *The Finnish Americans,* pp. 287-92.

5 Harold G. Moulton and Leo Pasvolsky, *War Debts and World Prosperity* (Washington, 1932), pp. 438-39; *New York Times,* December 6, 1939.

6 Thomas A. Bailey, *The Man in the Street* (New York, 1948), p. 236.

7 For conflicting studies of the role of non-Communist left-wing intellectuals in this period, see Eugene Lyons, *The Red Decade* (New York, 1941) and Granville Hicks, *Where We Came Out* (New York, 1954).

8 Meno Lovenstein, *American Opinion of Soviet Russia* (Washington, 1941), p. 158.

9 *Ibid.,* pp. 159-62.

10 Robert P. Browder, *Origins of Soviet-American Diplomacy* (Princeton, 1953), pp. 197-214.

11 United States Department of State, *Foreign Relations of the United States, the Soviet Union, 1933-1939* (Washington, 1943), pp. 457-91; Langer and Gleason, *Challenge to Isolation,* pp. 127-28; Hull, *Memoirs,* I, 657-58.

12 *New York Times,* August 24, 1939.

13 *The New Masses* (Vol. 33, No. 37, September 5, 1939), p. 4. Literary Editor Granville Hicks resigned his post in the same issue, calling the pact a "betrayal of the working class."

14 Diary of A.A. Berle, Jr., September 13, 18, as quoted in Langer and Gleason, *Challenge to Isolation,* p. 245.

15 Hull, *Memoirs,* I, 686-87.

16 *New York Times,* October 3, 1939.

17 Hull, *Memoirs,* I, 685.

18 Albin T. Anderson, "Origins of the Winter War" (*World Politics,* Vol. 6, No. 2, January, 1954), pp. 169-89; A. Rossi, *The Russo-German Alliance of 1939-1941* (London, 1950), p. 8; Raymond J. Sontag and James S. Beddie, *Nazi-Soviet Relations* (Washington, 1948), p. 2 *passim.*

19 *Documents Relating to the Eve of the Second World War* (New York, 1948), Vol. 2, "The Dirksen Papers," p. 183 ff.; Langer and Gleason, *Challenge to Isolation,* p. 107; *Nazi-Soviet Relations,* p. 36.

20 *Nazi-Soviet Relations,* pp. 32-36, 78, 105-7.

21 *Bulletin of International News* (Vol. 16, No. 2, June 17, 1939), p. 594; David J. Dallin, *Soviet Russia's Foreign Policy, 1939-1942* (New Haven, 1942), p. 80 ff.

22 John Wourinen, ed., *Finland and World War II* (New York, 1948), pp. 53-54; Finland, The Ministry of Foreign Affairs, *The Finnish Blue Book—the Development of Finnish-Soviet Relations During the Autumn of 1939 Including the Official Documents and Peace Treaty of March 12, 1940* (New York, 1940), pp. 46-49; Frederick L. Schuman, *Night Over Europe, 1939-1940* (New York, 1941), p. 399; *Foreign Relations of the United States, Soviet Union,* p. 974; Soviet Russia Today, *War and Peace in Finland* (New York, 1940), pp. 120-21, Ministry of Foreign Affairs for Finland, *Finnish White Book* (Helsinki, 1940), pp. 14-15.

23 Soviet Russia Today, *War and Peace in Finland,* p. 121; Wourinen, *Finland and World War II,* p. 59.

24 W.P. Coates and Z.K. Coates, *Russia, Finland and the Baltic* (London, 1940) pp. 104-5.

25 H.B. Elliston, *Finland Fights* (Boston, 1940), p. 212; *The Memoirs of Marshal Mannerheim* (London, 1953), p. 323.

26 Nancy Harvison Hooker, ed., *The Moffat Papers* (Cambridge, 1956), pp. 238-241.

27 Whitney H. Shepardson and William O. Scroogs, eds., *The United States in World Affairs, 1939* (New York, 1940), p. 279; United States Department of State, *Foreign Relations of the United States, Diplomatic Papers, 1939* (Washington, 1956), I, 954.

28 *Diplomatic Papers, 1939,* I, 956.

29 *Time* (Vol. 34, No. 17, October 23, 1939), p. 23; *New York Herald Tribune,* September 1, 1939.

30 *Diplomatic Papers, 1939,* I, 956-57.

31 Raymond Clapper in *New York World Telegram,* December 2, 1939.

32 *F.D.R.: His Personal Letters,* III, 880.

33 Hull, *Memoirs,* I, 743.

34 *Ibid.,* I, 702.

35 *Ibid.,* I, 703-4; *New York Times, Chicago Tribune,* October 9-30, 1939.

36 *The United States in World Affairs, 1939,* pp. 180-81.

37 *New York Times,* October 10, 1939.

38 Hooker, *Moffat Papers,* p. 270.

39 *Ibid.,* p. 271.

40 Hull, *Memoirs,* I, 702-3; *The Public Papers and Addresses of Franklin D. Roosevelt* (New York and Boston, 1938-1950), VIII, 538-39.

41 *Ibid.,* VIII, 539; Hull, *Memoirs,* I, 703-4; S. Shepard Jones and Denys P. Myers, ed., *Documents on American Foreign Relations, January, 1938-June, 1939* (Boston, 1939), p. 313.

42 *Finnish Blue Book,* p. 59; Mannerheim, *Memoirs,* p. 313; *New York Times,* November 1, 1939.

43 *New York Times, New York Daily News, Daily Worker, Chicago Tribune,* November 1-3, 1939.

44 Many newspapers and individuals observed that such incidents as the *City of Flint* affair would have been impossible under cash-and-carry.

45 As soon as the act was passed the Finns announced their plans to purchase 200 airplanes in the United States. Although F.D.R. would not help them directly, he admitted that "Finland has a perfect right to borrow money from American banks." *New York Daily News,* November 5, 1939; *New York Times,* November 14, 1939; *Christian Science Monitor,* November 17, 1939.

46 *New York Times,* October 12, 1939.

47 *New York Herald Tribune,* October 3, 1939; *Chicago Daily News,* October 14, 1939; *Chicago Tribune,* October 22, 1939.

48 *New York Daily News,* November 17, 1939.

49 Hull, *Memoirs,* I, 705-6; Dallin, *Soviet Russia's Foreign Policy,* p. 121.

50 Hooker, *Moffat Papers,* p. 280; Langer and Gleason, *Challenge to Isolation,* pp. 327-28.

51 *Berle Diaries,* November 29, 1939, as quoted in *Ibid.,* p. 328.

52 *New York Times,* November 28, 1939; Great Britain, Royal Institute of International Affairs, *Survey of International Affairs, 1939-1946,* Arnold Toynbee, ed., William Hardy McNeill, *America, Britain, and Russia: Their Cooperation and Conflict, 1941-1946* (London, 1953), p. 49; Winston Churchill, *The Gathering Storm* (Boston, 1948), pp. 422-23.

53 Hugh Gibson, ed., *The Ciano Diaries, 1939-1943* (Boston, 1946), pp. 174-75; *New York Times,* November 28, 1939.

54 *New York Times,* December 4, 1939.

55 *Business Week* (No. 530, October 28, 1939), p. 53; Shepardson and Scroogs, *The United States in World Affairs, 1940,* p. 24; Foster Rhea Dulles, *The Road to Teheran* (New York, 1947), p. 222.

56 *New York Times,* November 30, 1939; *Atlanta Constitution; Dallas Morning News; Cleveland Plain Dealer; Washington Evening Star,* December 1, 1939, as quoted in C.C. Tansill, *Back Door to War* (Chicago, 1952), p. 573.

57 *New York Herald Tribune,* December 2, 1939; *New York Mirror,* December 5, 1939.

58 *New York Herald Tribune,* December 3, 1939; *Chicago Tribune,* December 1, 1939.

59 *New York Herald Tribune,* December 6, 1939; An exception was Samuel Grafton of the *New York Post* who on December 7, wrote that although he sympathized with Finland, "Dead Americans won't bring dead Finns back to life."

60 Harold Lavine and James Wechsler, *War Propaganda and the United States* (New Haven, 1940), p. 286; *New York Times,* November 30, 1939; *New York Herald Tribune,* December 3, 1939; *New York Daily News,* December 1, 1939.

61 Ickes, *Secret Diary,* III, 75.

62 *London Times,* December 2, 1939.

Chapter V

THE ADMINISTRATION HESITATES

Official Washington made no attempt to disguise its pro-Finnish sympathies. Roosevelt spoke for the nation when he asserted that "all peace loving people . . . unanimously condemn (this) . . . resort to military force as an arbiter of international differences." When informed of the Soviet bombing of Helsinki the President was genuinely indignant; the news came as a "profound shock." "It is tragic," he said, "to see the policy of force spreading and to realize that wanton disregard for law is still on the march." [1] Roosevelt immediately sent appeals to Moscow and Helsinki asking the leaders of both nations not to bomb civilian populations. The Finns readily agreed, but Molotov, resenting the insinuation, categorically refused to take such a pledge. The Red Army, he said, had never and would never bomb civilian populations; Red airplanes were engaged in demolishing airdromes, not cities. The Commissar stated that the Soviet Union "is no less concerned for the interests of the Finnish population than any other government." In speaking to Ambassador Laurence Steinhardt, he observed that "one may fail to see this in America, over eight thousand kilometers away from Finland." Molotov told the American that "in view of this, the . . . statement by Mr. Roosevelt is obviously pointless." [2] The Russian made it clear that intervention in any form by Washington would be unwelcome by the Kremlin.

The Administration was at a loss as to what action to take in this crisis. The State Department was divided on the question of American European policy throughout the period. On the morning of the attack Hull sent for Under Secretary Sumner Welles, Moffat, and Stanley Hornbeck and James Dunn of the European Department. All agreed that the United States could not remain silent in the face of the Soviet attack. Hull told the group that he would prepare a strong public statement on the question. At this time Welles, whose outlook was often different from that of the Secretary, suggested that Hull be more positive in his actions; far more effective would be an announcement that the United States had broken diplomatic relations with the U.S.S.R. Viewing the Russo-Finnish War in a broader perspective than Hull, he argued that an act of this nature would show the German and Japanese imperialists where the United States stood on aggression, and might cause them to act in a more cautious manner in the future. Hull remained adamant. He doubted whether drastic actions would accomplish anything in the way of limiting the European wars and future hostilities in Asia. Although Welles persisted, and later tried to win Hornbeck and Moffat to his way of thinking, Hull's position was adopted as the official view of the Department. This breach was indicative not only of the growing rift between the two men, but also of the indicision in high policy circles in the Government.[3]

The President himself reflected these doubts. He seemed not to have made up his mind as how to act at this time. Would the war last but a few weeks, as most "experts" predicted? Was the attack a forerunner of an eventual Russo-German invasion of Scandinavia? Stalin gave no indication as to where or when the Red Army might next strike. Roosevelt was forced to play a waiting game, as he asked himself and others: "I wonder what the next Russian plan is?" [4]

As a result the Administration was unwilling and unable to take a strong stand. Roosevelt would lead the protests, but in so doing would try to speak as the voice of the American conscience, and not as the President or the Commander-in-Chief. Words spoken in Finland's behalf would not be backed by the full authority of the Executive office. Following this negative orientation, most of the official decisions involved acts of omission rather than commission. Roosevelt might discontinue practices which in the past had aided the Soviets, but he was not eager to impose new restrictions upon them.

In accord with this tenuous policy, Roosevelt expressed the hope that American manufacturers would stop the export of airplanes to nations which bombed civilian populations. Although the message could have applied to Japan, its timing made it evident that the President was referring to the Soviet Union.[5] Within the circle of the Cabinet, he brought up the possibility of a new moral embargo against the Soviets. On December 4, Roosevelt told Morgenthau to make sure that Moscow could not purchase aluminum in the United States. The Secretary replied that such a restriction would be most difficult, since the Soviets were not engaged in illegal practices of any kind. Perhaps recalling New Deal days, the President answered that more difficult problems had been solved in the past.[6] He apparently expected Morgenthau to do all he could under the existing laws. Roosevelt did not recommend the introduction of new legislation aimed specifically at the Soviets. The moral embargo was announced, and soon thereafter molybdenum, nickel, tungsten, and machinery were added to the list, but Morgenthau had no means at his disposal to enforce the President's wish other than his personal contacts with American manufacturers.[7]

The concept of moral embargoes was not new to the American scene. One had been applied during the Italo-Ethiopian War with little success.[8] The same fate was to greet its reintroduction in 1939. At the time of the outbreak of hostilities, nearly 300 firms in fifteen states had back orders from *Amtorg*. States in the northeastern quadrant of the nation, such as Pennsylvania, Ohio and New York, were among the most vocal in their denunciation of the Soviet aggression, but each of these states also averaged over $1 million worth of business with Soviet trade representatives during 1939.[9] Would the manufacturers involved allow their emotions to interfere with business? The answer was a resounding, almost unanimous, "NO." With the exception of one small machine tool company in Milwaukee these businesses took no heed of the moral embargo. Hundreds of businessmen engaged in this highly profitable trade watched each other for a possible break in their ranks. If one would publicly renounce his Soviet orders the others might be forced to follow. No such break occurred.[10] Although they mouthed platitudes about "Brave Little Finland," their motto was still "Business as Usual." Toward the end of December American fur buyers took practically the entire offering of the Soviet merchants. Total purchases were approximately $30 million, which was almost double that of the previous year.[11] Another example was the copper trade with the Soviet Union. On February 7, the Red tanker *Kim* discharged $5,600,000 worth of gold bullion at San Francisco, where it was used to redress the Soviet-American trade balance. At the same time, the American ship *Harpoon* was anchored in the Mexican port of Manzanillo, discharging a cargo of 8,000 tons of copper. During that week more copper arrived by rail to the port. Shortly thereafter the *Kim* docked at Manzanillo and loaded the metal for the trip back to Vladivostok. "If the transshipment of the cargo means anything," wrote an American business magazine, "it means that moral embargoes won't stick. Businessmen are likely to sell their wares regardless of artificial restrictions." [12]

The President did crack down on one industry, however. In the second half of 1939 some 1,300,000 barrels of gasoline were purchased by Soviet agents, and there was no indication that these shipments would be voluntarily stopped. Toward the end of January Roosevelt initiated indirect action against those engaged in this trade, instructing A. A. Berle, Jr. to contact the Maritime Commission and inform them that in the future oilers bound for Soviet ports would be stopped, using "good and sufficient reasons." [13] The scheme worked, and constituted the first and only success in stopping the Soviet trade. In February, however, private sources reported that Moscow had purchased $2,200,000 worth of oil drilling machinery in the United States.[14] The total effect was rather bizarre. With one hand American petroleum was withheld, while the other aided the Soviets in developing their own resources to compensate for the loss!

In reviewing the role of American business, Thomas J. Watson, President of International Business Machines, announced that he and his colleagues in private industry were actively cooperating with the President "in a great effort in doing our part in a cause that is vital to all industry—the defeat of Communism." [15] Such were the words—and the actions.

When news of the War reached the United States many believed that the President would take the opportunity to test the strength of the Neutrality Act. The legislation was now more to the Administration's liking and Roosevelt had openly expressed satisfaction with the results of the special session. Thus, it might well be considered an act of bad faith for the President not to invoke the Neutrality Act. There were, however, extenuating circumstances which again illustrated the futility of any attempt to legislate neutrality.

In the first place, neither the Soviet Union nor Finland had declared war. Had the President found a state of war to exist—as was well within his rights to do—he would have had to apply the rule of cash-and-carry to both nations. Since Finland had no navy to speak of, this would have resulted in an effectual embargo on that nation. At the same time, all negotiations for special credits would have to be halted. In any case, even without a declaration of war, American shipping was prevented from entering the Baltic by restrictions imposed during the European war. If Finland were to get American goods of any description, they would have to be transported in foreign bottoms.

Most important, however, was that policy which guided Soviet-American relations. Roosevelt and Hull had no desire to take any action which might lead to a further strengthening of the Nazi-Soviet tie; declaring the U.S.S.R. a belligerent might easily have had such an effect.[16] This policy was further strengthened by dispatches from the American embassies abroad. On December 30 Steinhardt cabled from Moscow one of several such notices:

> Councelor of the French Embassy told me yesterday in strict confidence that he and his Ambassador had come to the conclusion that the German Government is desirous of seeing a rupture of diplomatic relations between France, Great Britain, and the United States and the Soviet Union, because of the obvious advantages to Germany which would result therefrom.[17]

Hull's actions were such as to give Stalin little reason to complain of American interference. When asked by the Finns to extend American good offices for the settlement of the war, Hull noted that he was in a situation which was "most embarrassing." In his instructions to Steinhardt on December 2 regarding the Ambassador's answers to such requests, Hull stated that he

> should explain to the Minister that we feel that Finnish interests could most effectively be protected by the Italian Ambassador, who has apparently indicated a willingness to accept the task. You may add, however that if at any time we could informally be of help to the Italian Ambassador, you would be glad to cooperate.[18]

This episode illustrated the American attitude. As Hull later wrote:

> I could not but feel that the basic antagonisms between Communist Russia and Nazi Germany were so deep, and Hitler's ambition so boundless, that eventually Russia would come over to the side of the Allies. We had to be careful not to push her in the other direction.[19]

Hull's realism was to be vindicated the following year, when Hitler attacked the Soviet Union. While others were calling for a severance of relations with Moscow, the Secretary considered that one day the U.S.S.R. would be needed in the battles against Germany. When Roosevelt seemed to falter, his natural sympathies for the Finns leading him to advocate a program of aid for that nation, Hull's counsels were heeded, and the disasterous consequences of such a move were averted. When the majority of Congress, including the non-interventionists, declared itself pro-Finnish, Hull was able to keep a calm head. His was the only voice in the Administration or Congress that did not change with the vicissitudes of political expediency. He was in favor of international cooperation when Roosevelt dynamited the London Conference of 1933, and he remained in that camp throughout the isolationist days of the early New Deal. Hull was in favor of co-ordinated action by democratic states to preserve peace long before Litvinov began to expound the doctrine of a united front against fascism. When his internationalist leanings might have led him to advocate positive aid to Finland, Hull had the wisdom and foresight to realize that the War was but a minor diversion from the greater European conflict. While others shifted their attentions to Moscow and Helsinki, Hull remained primarily concerned with London and Berlin. He was not a complex individual, which was all for the good in this situation. In concentrating on the more important international problems of the day he did his country and the world the greatest service it was in the power of an American Secretary of State to do.

With the failure of the moral embargo and the inability to use the Neutrality Act against the Soviet Union, the United States was still faced with the problem of how to aid the Finns. The most obvious methods appeared to be an American loan and private donations which would enable the Finns to buy war supplies in America. Since Finland had paid her debts, the provisions of the Johnson Act did not extend to her. An official loan could also be granted. This plan soon gained popularity; give Finland money so that she could purchase the necessary arms in the United States. One of the first moves in this direction was the recommendation that Finland's debt payment, which would soon fall due, be discontinued. Roosevelt was evasive as to what would be done with the Finnish check. The question came up at the press conference of December 5. Would the money be turned back to the Finns so that they could use it to buy war supplies? The President side-stepped the issue, saying that "there are lots of ways it could be used in a perfectly neutral way." [20] He then declined to discuss the matter further. Though unwilling at this time to step out of the bounds of existing legislation, Roosevelt instructed Morgenthau to place the payment in a special fund.[21] In a letter to a friend who favored aid to Finland, the President stated that although he was considered "a benevolent dictator and an all powerful Santa Claus," his office operated "under the laws which the all-wise Congress passes." "Whether we like it or not," he wrote, "Congress and God still live." While they did, Roosevelt—perhaps the strongest of all American presidents—would not usurp their powers.[22] When Ickes suggested a moratorium on the Finnish debt, the President replied that Congress would have to take action before this could be done. Roosevelt was also silent on Ickes' suggestion that the payment be used to purchase airplanes and munitions for the Finns.[23] The press was responsive to the idea, and favored many schemes which would, in effect, return the money to Finland.[24] We should say to Finland, "for the duration of your splendid struggle, in which you have the fullest American sympathy, Keep your Money." [25]

The second possibility was a direct loan to Finland. On December 5, Procope conferred with Jesse Jones, the Administrator of the Reconstruction Finance Corporation, who suggested that a private company might be organized with American and Finnish subscriptions at a ratio of five to one. This corporation would then receive credits from the R.F.C. to purchase American goods such as wheat and cotton, which would be sold in Liverpool for pounds. After the necessary currency conversions, the money thus gained could be spent in the United States for arms and munitions.[26] Although this plan fell through, five days later Jones announced that a loan of $10 million had been granted Finland through the Export-Import Bank, the financial arm of the R.F.C.[27] The money was most welcome, but in retrospect seems to have done the Finns more harm than good. It was stipulated that the credits could be used only in the purchase of agricultural surplusses, and that the United States would not aid in their marketing abroad. In this way the real need —guns, planes, munitions—had been bypassed through the use of an agency designed to deal with problems of a peaceful nature. Yet those who favored granting aid to Finland without agitating Soviet-American relations could claim that, by so acting, the United States had discharged its moral obligation in full.

The question of a loan through another agency for the purchase of military supplies was mentioned by some students of the problem, but the legality of such an action under the provisions of the Hague Neutrality Convention was questionable.[28] Again, the nature of belligerent rights rose to cloud the issue. In any case, it was evident that Roosevelt, in pursuing his policy of caution, would not consent to underwrite such a program without the full consent and concurrence of Congress. He thought that a loan of this nature could not be considered, and even doubted the possibility of a new loan by the R.F.C. He confided to Hull a "fear that we cannot make any large loan to Finland under the R.F.C. act, because, frankly, there is not enough security for its repayment under the existing law."[29]

In the meanwhile the Finns negotiated for the purchase of American arms, drawing upon deposits in New York banks which had accumulated during the interwar period. In the first month of the War the Finnish Legation placed more than $3 million worth of orders with American firms.[30] On December 18 Secretary of the Navy Charles Edison announced that forty Brewster fighter planes of the latest design had been purchased by Helsinki. The Secretary stressed the fact that the United States Government had nothing at all to do with the transaction, which was a private matter between the Brewster Corporation and the Finns. These dealings were strictly business, and "it is understood . . . that cash is being paid for all such supplies."[31] Nevertheless the American Army did cooperate to a limited extent. The War Department arranged for the visit to the United States of Villio P. Nenonen, the commander of

Finland's artillery and a leading ordinance expert. The General toured American factories in late December, stating "it is only in the United States that we can get adequate supplies." [32] Soon he was arranging for the purchase of trench mortars, anti-tank guns, and ammunition.[33] Despite the half-hearted opposition of Hull, who thought this policy to be most unneutral, the Government cooperated with Nenonen throughout the War.[34]

On December 1, Senator King of Utah called on the President to commend him on his rapid reply to the Soviet attack. Roosevelt was assured of King's support in such actions.[35] Other such messages were received by the White House throughout the War. Meetings to protest Russian brutality and applaud Finland were held from one end of the nation to the other. In Hollywood more than a score of celebrities gathered at a huge "Help Finland" rally, while in New York, Alexander Kerensky and Thomas Mann addressed more than 2,000 people who had crowded into a small ballroom in downtown Manhattan to cheer the Finns and hiss the Kremlin. The Administration gave its approval to such demonstrations and aided Hendrik Van Loon, the writer, in the preparation of a large rally in Madison Square Garden.[36]

Senator King and Representative Dies recommended that this country break diplomatic relations with the Soviet Union. When asked of the possibility of such a move, Roosevelt refused to comment.[37] At this time the Soviets had violated their agreement to abide by the principle of reciprocity in the treatment of diplomatic personnel. Yet it was obvious that Roosevelt had no intention of taking drastic actions in the situation. Looking back at the Administration's reactions to the War in its first month, one can find little of a positive nature, with the exception of the first R.F.C. loan, which had been attempted. The United States had expressed indignation, had imposed an ineffectual moral embargo, had refused to use the Neutrality Act, and had delayed the granting of military credits to Finland. Caution was the byword in December of 1939, and this caution extended throughout the duration of the War. Indeed, public figures and legislators alike seemed to avoid the problem. The "great debate" on foreign policy had taken place over the revision of the Neutrality Act, and had been won by the Administration which still treaded carefully in foreign affairs. The result of the debate was more a victory for presidential discretion and limited economic aid to the Allies than a defeat for noninterventionism. The trend toward that doctrine had been halted, but Congress had not yet turned in the direction of interventionism. "Isolation today is Congress-wide," wrote one influential publication, "and the White House knows it." [38] Roosevelt thought that the United States should "match every Soviet annoyance by a similar treatment here against them," and, as Hull wrote, "these minor irritations from Russia continued to rankle in the President's mind." [39] It soon became evident, however, that Roosevelt would not support those extremists who would have him recall the embassy in Moscow, as had been done under similar circumstances in the case of Germany. "As Congress sees it, the President is content for the present to take sides, but is limiting his activities to methods short of war."[40] The Administration refused to comment on the proposed military loan to Finland; as 1940 was to be a critical election year, it was evidently felt that the issue would be "too hot to handle."[41]

Still, it had become increasingly difficult to steer the tenuous middle course—to maintain an aloof relationship with Moscow in order to demonstrate American disapproval and at the same time not to alienate the Kremlin and destroy the possibility of *rapprochement*. On the one hand Roosevelt called the U.S.S.R. "a dictatorship as absolute as any other dictatorship in the world," while on the other General Krivitsky, the former head of Soviet Military Intelligence whose testimony before the Dies Committee was embarrassing to Moscow, was told that he had to leave the country by December 31.[42] Although the Administration did not embark on a program of attrition against the Soviet Union, there were many minor incidents which served as a gauge to the official attitude. On December 16, *Booknιga* Incorporated of New York, the American agent for a Soviet publishing house, and three of its officers, were indicted on charges of conspiracy and violation of the Foreign Agents Registration Act.[43] While Congress debated the Finnish loan, Earl Browder, Secretary of the American Communist Party, was found guilty of traveling on a passport obtained by false statements, and was sentenced to four years in jail.[44] Perhaps the most significant move of the month was Roosevelt's announcement that Americans could volunteer for the Finnish Army and still retain their citizenship.[45]

The Soviets on their part criticized the Administration for its "unfriendly" and "warlike" acts. *Red Star* charged that "reaction is growing in the United States," citing as an example "the prosecution of Communists." America, it charged, had embarked on a "dark, dirty game as dealers of death."[46] *Komsomolskaya Pravda* predicted that these policies would end in the United States being drawn into the World War.[47] The reaction against the United States was such that Steinhardt, in a cable to Hull on December 31, reported:

> I have no evidence which would justify the opinion that the present time is propitious to approach the Soviet Government for the purpose of bringing about negotiations with the Finnish Government, nor is there as yet any sign of a desire on the part of the Soviet Government to extricate itself from the difficulties which it has encountered in the prosecution of the war with Finland.[48]

However, the Kremlin realized that the United States had no intention of interfering any more than was necessary in the European conflicts. Indeed, Roosevelt thought so little of the Russo-Finnish War that he left the country early in February for a cruise. While Congress was debating the Finnish loan, he sunned himself in Florida; while the vote was taken on the legislation, the President reviewed the forces at the Canal Zone. Roosevelt did not return to the United States until February 28, when the congressional battles were over and the War had entered its final stages.[49]

Thus, the Administration played but a minor role during the War. The complex problems of isolationism, combined with the simple truth that the World War had to take precedence over the Winter War in American planning, prevented Roosevelt from pursuing any other course of action. If the Government would not grant more positive aid, however, perhaps the American people, who had expressed their admiration and support for Finland in the past, could be counted upon.

NOTES

Chapter V: THE ADMINISTRATION HESITATES

1 *New York Times,* December 2, 1939; United States Department of State, *Bulletin,* Series II, No. 295, March 16, 1940.

2 *The U.S.S.R. and Finland,* p. 35; Dallin, *Soviet Russia's Foreign Policy,* p. 143.

3 Hooker, *Moffat Papers,* pp. 280-81.

4 Letter from Roosevelt to Lincoln MacVeagh, Minister to Greece, on December 1, 1939, *Roosevelt Papers.*

5 American companies were asked by the Government to recall engineers who had been on loan to the Soviet Union. *New York Times,* December 3, 1939; Hull, *Memoirs,* Vol. I, pp. 706-7.

6 Ickes, *Secret Diary,* Vol. III, p. 75.

7 Hull, *Memoirs,* Vol. I, p. 707; *Morgenthau Diaries,* December 15, 1939, as cited in Langer and Gleason, *Challenge to Isolation,* p. 331.

8 Hull, *Memoirs,* Vol. I, pp. 432-33; United States House of Representatives, Foreign Affairs Committee, 74th Congress, 2nd Session, *To Maintain the Neutrality of the United States in the Event of War Between or Among Foreign Nations* (H.J. Resolution 422) (Washington, 1936), p. 17 ff.; *Department of Commerce New Release,* November 23, 1935.

9 The states which had the largest portion of the Soviet trade during 1939, and their gross business, were:

Pennsylvania	$12,496,100
Ohio	11,656,900
New York	11,041,700
New Jersey	6,754,500
Colorado	6,650,000

Source: *Business Week* (No. 547, February 24, 1940), p. 59.

10 *Ibid.* (No. 543, January 27, 1940), p. 62.

11 *Ibid.* (No. 538, December 30, 1939), p. 31.

12 *New York Times,* February 21, 1940; *Business Week* (No. 545, February 10, 1940), p. 55; *New York World Telegram,* February 9, 1940.

13 Memorandum from Roosevelt to Berle, and Berle to Roosevelt, January 27, February 1, 1940, *Roosevelt Papers.*

14 *Business Week* (No. 543, January 27, 1940), p. 62; *New York Times,* February 22, 1940.

15 *Ibid.,* January 1, 1940.

16 *United States in World Affairs, 1940,* p. 27.

17 United States, *Diplomatic Papers,* 1939, p. 477.

18 *Ibid.,* p. 1017.

19 Hull, *Memoirs,* Vol. I, p. 707.

20 *Public Papers of Franklin Roosevelt,* Vol. VIII, pp. 590-94.

21 The total payment was $234,693.00. Hull, *Memoirs,* Vol. I, p. 707.

22 Roosevelt to Herbert Bayard Swope, December 4, 1939, in *F.D.R.: His Personal Letters,* Vol. III, p. 964.

23 Ickes, *Secret Diary,* Vol. III, pp. 80-81.

24 *New York Times,* December 4, 1939; *Chicago Daily News, New York Daily News,* December 7, 1939.

25 *Chicago Tribune,* December 7, 1939.

26 *New York Times,* December 6, 1939.

27 *New York Herald Tribune,* December 11, 1939.

28 For a discussion of this problem, see Charles C. Fenwick, *American Neutrality: Trail and Failure* (New York, 1940), especially pp. 107-8, 146.

29 Memorandum from Roosevelt to Hull, January 2, 1940, in *Roosevelt Papers.*

30 *Business Week* (No. 546, February 17, 1940), p. 55.

31 *New York Times,* December 19, 1939.

32 *Christian Science Monitor,* December 23, 1939.

33 *New York Post,* December 27, 1939.

34 The fact that Welles supported these policies further deepened the animosity between these two State Department leaders. Hooker, *Moffat Papers,* pp. 290-91.

35 Steve Early to Roosevelt, December 1, 1939, *Roosevelt Papers.*

36 *New York Times,* December 13, 1939; Van Loon to Early, December 11, 1939, Early to Van Loon, December 12, 1939, *Roosevelt Papers.* The President aided in obtaining Senator Robert Wagner of New York as a speaker for the rally.

37 *Public Papers of Franklin D. Roosevelt,* Vol. VIII, pp. 594-95.

38 *U.S. News,* February 2, 1940, p. 12.

39 Hull, *Memoirs,* Vol. I, pp. 708-10.

40 *U.S. News,* January 12, 1940, p. 43.

41 Ludwell Denny in *New York World Telegram,* January 17, 1940.

42 *New York Times,* January 17, 19, 1940.

43 *New York Post,* December 16, 1939.

44 *Ibid.,* January 22, 1940. Browder was later fined $2,000 in addition to this sentence.

45 *Ibid.,* January 26, 1940.

46 As quoted in *New York World Telegram,* December 16, 1939.

47 As quoted in *New York Times,* December 13, 1939.

48 United States, *Diplomatic Papers,* 1939, p. 1038.

49 *New York Times,* February 15, 18, 19, 1940; *New York Post,* February 18, 22, 27, 1940.

Chapter VI

THE PUBLIC AND THE PRESS

Roosevelt was more interventionist than the mass of the American people early in 1939. With the coming of the Winter War, however, the roles were reversed; the public response to the Finnish cause alarmed many Administration interventionists who feared that the open partisanship demonstrated in December might cause a breach in Soviet-American relations. Within days after the Soviet attack more than a dozen special interest groups had organized in behalf of Finland. The National Ski Association announced a coast-to-coast drive for funds, while the National Lutheran Council organized an appeal for $500,000 for civilian rehabilitation.[1] In Finnish relief, however, such special organizations played a secondary role. Unlike French, Polish, Spanish, and Chinese aid organizations, economic, religious and political factors were lacking. With the exception of unorganized opposition from some radicals, aid to Finland was supported by all elements of the population and all sections of the nation.[2]

The near universal acceptance and support of the Finnish cause was reflected in the activities of the Finnish Relief Fund, which was headed by Herbert Hoover. Although the ex-President had turned down Administration offers of similar posts, he readily accepted the chairmanship of this drive.[3] Characterizing the Soviet attack as "a throwback to the morals and butchery of Genghiz Khan," he travelled widely to unite the public behind Finnish relief.[4] All of Hoover's aides were volunteers, which made it possible for the Fund to turn over more than 90% of its collections to the Finns.[5] December 17 was designated as "Finland Day," and appropriate observances, speeches and parades were held throughout the nation. New York's Finland Day saw the public paying as high as $100 for a box at Madison Square Garden to see Hoover clasp hands with Fiorello LaGuardia, Dorothy Thompson, and Senator Robert Wagner, all interventionists who had been less than friendly to the ex-President in the past.[6] "Nights for Finland" were staged in Chicago, Los Angeles, Denver and St. Louis.[7] Small towns participated; the Fund received a $1,750 check from the proceeds of a meeting held in Eldorado, Arkansas.[8] Rare was the individual "who had neither danced, knitted, orated, played bridge, bingo, banqueted, or just shelled out for Finland." By March 15, over $3,500,000 had been collected by the Fund and turned over to Finnish Relief.[9]

The money collected by the Fund was used to purchase food, medical supplies, and other items to aid in civilian rehabilitation. The more pressing need, that of military supplies, was neglected by the Hoover group. The Chairman seemed intent on filling the same role in 1940 as he had in 1915. In an address delivered toward the end of January, Hoover stated that "America *must not* join this European war . . . but the American people can give their help to the civilian population." [10]

Hoover's refusal to use Fund collections to purchase munitions for Finland created an awkward situation. "Mr. Hoover may well ask himself what use it is to organize Finnish relief if Finland is not helped to resist," wrote one commentator.[11] The need for such military aid sparked the formation of "Fighting Funds for Finland." Headed by Major General John O'Ryan, former commander of the famed 27th division of World War I, the organization pledged itself to the collection of military funds only. O'Ryan appealed to those Americans of a more militant stripe who perhaps hoped to use the Finnish conflict as a lever in attempting to involve the United States directly in the World War.[12] Although the General collected less than a million dollars during his ill-organized drive, it did cause Hoover to accept donations for military purposes also. By the end of the War, the Fund had become infiltrated with interventionists.[13] As the mood filtered down to the mass of American people, so it percolated up to the White House. F.D.R. received hundreds of letters and telegrams urging a more militant Administration role in the War. A woman in Denver offered to sell her home and donate the proceeds to Finnish relief if the Government would match her dollar for dollar, and a professional wolf catcher from Los Angeles suggested that the Government hire the Los Angeles Coliseum for an exhibition of his skills, with the gate receipts going to Finland.[14]

The newspapers fanned this wave of pro-Finnish sentiment. More than 1,200 newspapers aided the Hoover Fund by acting as collection agents for Finnish donations, and publishers Roy Howard and Arthur Hays Sulzburger were on the Fund's Board of Directors.[15] The Winter War made good copy, and the press played it up with such headlines as "Finns Riddle Soviet Mass Attack . . . Finns Smash Big Red Attack . . . 30,000 Russians Reported Killed."[16] There were reports of a clash between the Red and Finnish fleets and a battle in which two Soviet armies were surrounded. The press set Soviet casualties at a quarter of a million.[17] Unfortunately for Finland, none of these events actually occurred. There was no Finnish fleet to speak of, and the Finns had hardly enough men to surround a division, much less two armies.

The *Chicago Tribune* reported that the Finns had wiped out a Soviet parachute army, and a noted columnist talked of 100 Finns who had stood off 300,000 Red soldiers.[18] Throughout the War the Soviets were accused of using gas.[19] When reporting on guerrilla fighting, one observer commented:

> By the second week of January the campaign was over. Thirty-six thousand Russians were dead and all their supplies were captured. The total number of Finnish lives lost is believed to have been less than one hundred and fifty.[20]

When the casualties reported in the first five weeks of fighting were tabulated, it was discovered that the usually sober *New York Times* had reported 55,537 Red deaths as against 269 Finns.[21]

One reason for these wild reports was a desire to sell newspapers that goes back at least to the Spanish-American War. Another was the fact that the editors, in common with their fellow-citizens, were overwhelmingly pro-Finnish and anti-Soviet. News reports became thinly disguised editorials in their hands, and the line between fact and opinion was disregarded. In addition, the fighting on the western front had subsided into the "Phoney War" by this time, and the fighting in the North served to satisfy a public which expected war news on its front pages.

But despite the inactivity in the West, the seasoned reporters remained in France on the chance that a break-through might take place. As a result, only less qualified men could be spared to cover the Finnish campaign.[22] The *New York Herald Tribune* did not have a special observer in Helsinki until late in January, and the *Los Angeles Times* and *Atlanta Constitution* reported the War from London sources. The *Detroit Free Press, Cincinnati Enquirer* and *Dallas Morning News* relied almost exclusively upon the wire services, as did other major newspapers.

The Finnish communications system didn't help in the coverage. Helsinki had but two radio stations and each had less than two kilowatts of power.[23] Broadcasting over either was extremely difficult and, in the beginning of the War, impossible. Later on reports were broadcast to Stockholm, relayed to London, and then finally to the United States. To this was added the problem of transportation. In order to get to the front lines reporters had to know how to ski, and no American reporter in Finland could. As a result the newsmen would congregate in Helsinki's Hotel Kamp and Hotel Torni and swap stories, many of which had no foundation but nonetheless would appear on the front pages of American papers.[24] Sometimes the Americans could wring a story from Swedish newsmen, who could translate Finnish communiques for them. No American reporter in Finland at this time could read or speak Finnish. Faced with a lack of information, rumors, half-truths and exaggeration, the often inexperienced reporters concocted weird tales which a gullable American public accepted as gospel.[25]

The major wire services were little better. The *United Press* was the most reliable, its stories usually agreeing with later accounts. The *Associated Press* had the most correspondents in Finland, but it concentrated on "human interest" stories of Finnish bravery and did a generally poor job on the War itself. The *International News Service* was frankly sensationalist. Most of its stories eminated from Copenhagen, miles from the scene of action. I.N.S. reported gas attacks that never took place and air raids dreamed up in their reporter's imaginations. This service was also responsible for the mystery story of the War, which concerned the "Nenonen formula" for artillery firing, called "the key reason for the Finnish successes." [26]

None of the reporters were at the front in December, but this did not prevent them from writing as though they were battling side by side with the Finnish troops. Not until the last week in January did the Americans visit a battlefield.[27] One reporter stated that "old time newspaper correspondents say that the war in Finland was the first war in many years without war correspondents."[28] "No American correspondent has ever remained long at the front" wrote Leland Stowe, who admitted that first hand news was scarce although his reports led one to believe that he was in the middle of the action at all times.[29]

As a result of this misinformation, most Americans believed that Finland was at least holding its own, if not actually winning against the Red Army. This tended to heighten the pro-Finnish and anti-Soviet sentiments which already existed. "This country is more ready for war with the Soviet Union than with Germany," wrote *Common Sense*. "In contrast to our realism toward one war, we are sentimental, even hysterical, toward another." [30]

Although this observation seemed well based in view of the situation as it appeared in early 1940, it should be remembered that most Americans did not want to fight either Germany or the Soviet Union. The first rash of indignation at the Soviet attack was followed by an isolationist period of second thoughts. The *New Republic* wrote that "there has never been a clearer case of calculated and unprovoked aggression by a larger power against a small neighbor than the invasion of Finland by the Soviet Union." [31] This does not mean, however, that the United States need go to war to avenge this crime; Finland should be helped by her neighbors, not by this country. "When it is clear that Finland has received all possible help from her European friends and still needs more, it will be time—if ever—to consider accepting the risk." [32] George V. Denney, Jr., moderator of the popular Town Hall Meeting of the Air, a radio program designed to feel the pulse of the nation, reported that "there is little or no sentiment for American intervention in Finland's behalf." Americans who wrote to him were almost unanimous in their belief that America should stay out of war.[33] The *New York Journal and American*, one of the leading jingo newspapers in the nation, editorially rejected suggestions of American aid to Finland at the same time as it published stories designed to inflame opinion in behalf of Finnish aid.[34] The Veterans of Foreign Wars and American Legion followed the same line. "There's plenty of crusading to be done here at home" opined the V.F.W.[35]

The non-interventionists of the right were joined by non-interventionists of the left. Theodore Dreiser, then the leading literary spokesman of the non-Communist left, stated that he would have supported Finnish aid provided there had been a similar movement for the Spanish Republic. Why help semi-facist Finland, he argued, when we did not help Abyssinia or China against their totalitarian enemies? Dreiser linked pro-Finnish Americans with anti-liberalism, and refused to join movements in behalf of Finland.[36] So important a figure as Harold Ickes wondered whether it was right to aid Finland, considering the strong Germanic connections of that nation. To him Marshal Mannerheim was an aristocrat who had suppressed the Finnish peasantry, a man who was supported by and would in the future aid "the aristocratic and monied interests of England and France" [37]

The non-Communist left, still thinking perhaps of the days when Litvinov spoke of a United Front and asked for a union of anti-fascist nations to safeguard peace, found it difficult to brand the U.S.S.R. as an aggressor. The same individuals who spoke for war against Hitler because of his attack on Poland refused to consider war against Stalin for his attack on Finland. Their similarity to the isolationists, who opposed all interference with Europe, was one of the strangest sights of 1940. The *New Republic* and Charles Coughlin agreed on foreign policy while being diametrically opposed on all other issues. Communists like Earl Browder quoted anti-Communists like Charles Beard on the devil theory of war.[38] Both were forced to agree with Hull's program of non-intervention in the Winter War. And yet, all three—Hull, Browder, and Beard—though united on this question, disagreed as to the reasons for their actions. For Hull, aid to Finland might mean that the U.S.S.R. would be permanently lost to the Western Allies. Browder supported the Soviets for ideological reasons, shifting from the interventionism of 1938 to non-interventionism in 1939 with amazing ease. Beard opposed all forms of involvement as detrimental to American interests. Disagreeing with them were the vast majority of Americans, who wanted to "do something" for Finland but at the same time were unwilling to make a definite commitment. The *Milwaukee Journal*[39] presented the unpalatable choice in an editorial remarkable for the times in its candor:

> So we might have to face this question. There is no dodging. We might as well stop beating around the bush. Either we abandon our neutrality and become the ally of Finland or we do not meet the Finnish needs and requests. And if we do abandon our neutrality we have no idea or assurances of where we will stop.

If action were to be taken, it would have to be accomplished in Congress. Roosevelt had purposely vacillated. The public was leaderless and chaotic in their cries for Finnish aid. With this in mind, the *Atlanta Constitution* wrote that "this session is not merely window-dressing for the coming campaign. The Congress may be called upon to make decisions on the pressing matters of international concern." [40] F.D.R. had passed the buck, an unusual move for the strong President. Would Congress know what to do with it?

NOTES

Chapter VI: THE PUBLIC AND THE PRESS

1 *New York Times,* January 14, February 1, 1940.

2 *Ibid.,* January 1, 1940.

3 Ickes, *Secret Diary,* III, 12; *Newsweek* (Vol. XIV, No. 27, December 25, 1929), pp. 12-13.

4 *Chicago Tribune,* December 6, 1939.

5 Finnish Relief Fund, Inc. *Report to American Donors, December, 1939-July, 1940* (New York, 1949).

6 *New York Times,* December 19, 21, 1939.

7 *Ibid.,* February 28, 1940.

8 *Life* (Vol. 8, No. 11, February 13, 1940), p. 8.

9 *Time* (Vol. 35, No. 11, March 11, 1940), p. 16; *New York Times,* February 22, 1940.

10 *Ibid.,* January 28, 1940.

11 Walter Lippman in *New York Herald Tribune,* December 14, 1939. F.D.R. saw this column, and scrawled across it: "Ain't this a sock in the snoot for Herby the Hoot." *Roosevelt Papers.*

12 *New York Times,* February 2, 1940; Lavine and Wechsler, *War Propaganda and the United States,* pp. 298-99.

13 *Business Week* (No. 545, February 1, 1940), p. 62; *New York Times,* February 12, 20, 24, 1940.

14 Letter from Jack Abernathy to F.D.R. dated January 12, 1940, in *Roosevelt Papers.*

15 *New York Times,* December 12, 1939.

16 *New York World Telegram,* December 9, 20, 22, 1939.

17 *New York Daily News,* December 6, 9, 1939; January 1, 11; February 1, 6, 1940.

18 *Chicago Tribune,* December 2, 7, 16, 29, 31, 1939; Leland Stowe in *New York Post,* February 27, 1940.

19 *Chicago Tribune,* January 13, 1940.

20 Langdon-Davies, *Invasion in the Snow,* p. 42.

21 Tabulations cover the period of the War to January 8, 1940. *New Masses* (Vol. 24, No. 3, January 9, 1940), p. 5.

22 Hooper, *Through Soviet Russia,* p. 104.

23 Alton Cook in *New York World Telegram,* December 1, 1939. In order to reach the United States, over 100 kilowatts would have been needed.

24 Langdon-Davies, *Invasion in the Snow,* p. 43.

25 Don Eskelund in *New York Times,* January 17, 1940.

26 Leland Stowe in *Chicago Daily News,* December 8, 1939. The I.N.S. was charged with faking news photos to "expose" the Soviet bombings of civilian areas—attacks which never took place. Lavine and Wechsler, *War Propaganda and the United States,* p. 309 ff.

27 Coates and Coates, *Soviet-Finnish Campaign,* p. 9.

28 Walter Kerr in *New York Herald Tribune,* February 3, 1940.

29 Marcus Diffield and Bertram Zilmer, as quoted in "Newsmen Report the Finnish War," *Editor and Publisher,* Vol. 73, No. 2, January 13, 1940), p. 3; Leland Stowe in *Chicago Daily News,* February 5, 1940.

30 "On Hating Russia" (*Common Sense,* Vol. 9, No. 3, March, 1940), pp. 16-17. Hysteria was such that Cambridge, Massachusetts banned all books containing the name of V.I. Lenin or Leningrad, and the A.F.L. issued a boycott against all Soviet-made goods. A group of New Yorkers suggested that the Police Department turn over all captured firearms to the Finns. Lavine and Wechsler, *War Propaganda and the United States,* p. 287; *New York Times,* January 6, February 21, 1940.

31 "Stalin Spreads the War" (*New Republic,* Vol. 101, No. 1306, December 13, 1939), p. 218.

32 *Ibid.* (Vol. 102, No. 5, January 29, 1940), p. 132.

33 George V. Denney, Jr., "What Aid for Finland?" (*Current History,* Vol. 51, No. 7, March, 1940), p. 43.

34 *New York Journal and American,* December 20, 1939.

35 *New York Times,* February 26, 1940; *National Legionaire,* March, 1940.

36 *New Masses* (Vol. 34, No. 6, January 30, 1940), p. 8. Also see *Between Dives and Lazarus,* unpublished mss. on deposit in New York Public Library.

37 Ickes, *Secret Diary,* III, 134.

38 Soviet Russia Today, *War and Peace in Finland,* pp. 32-33.

39 *Milwaukee Journal,* February 2, 1940.

40 *Atlanta Constitution,* December 29, 1939.

Chapter VII

CONGRESSIONAL ACTION

Congress reconvened on January 3, at a time when pro-Finnish sentiment was strongest and Soviet defeats dominated the headlines. A small Finnish force invaded Soviet territory on Christmas Day, and the news of this "counter-attack" set off a new wave of demands for American aid to that nation.[1]

This public interest, which Roosevelt would have welcomed had it been for Anglo-French aid, proved embarrassing to the President as he addressed the joint session. He omitted all reference to the Russo-Finnish War and claimed ignorance of congressional plans for assistance to Finland when questioned about them later on.[2]

The vacuum left by F.D.R.'s abdication of leadership was filled by eastern internationalists and mid-western isolationists who had to placate their large Scandinavian constituencies. Celler of New York and Hook and Dingall of Michigan proposed that the United States aid Finland with shipments of guns, planes and munitions,[3] but the most important proposal in terms of general interest came from Senator Prentiss Brown of Michigan, an isolationist who accepted interventionism when World War II began. Brown proposed that the Reconstruction Finance Corporation lend Finland up to $60 million, which would be used to purchase materials Finland deemed necessary to conduct the War. Under the loose wording of Brown's draft, the Finns could purchase a large amount of war material in the United States. Realizing that such a drastic plan would meet with strong non-interventionist opposition, Brown added a provision which stated that the capitalization of the Export-Import Bank, the fiscal agent of the R.F.C., would be increased from $100 million to $200 million, and that all loans from the Bank would be used for non-military purposes.[4] This draft meant all things to all people. It was publicized as a bill to aid Finland without endangering American neutrality, and as such won the support of many congressmen who hadn't the foggiest notion of what it contained. Senator Ashurst of Arizona was more honest than most when he asked, after weeks of discussion, whether a vote for the Brown Bill meant a vote for Finnish aid. "I intend to be a candidate for reelection to the Senate," he said, "and beyond any doubt I shall be asked whether or not I voted for the loan to Finland." [5] Brown assured him that a vote for his proposal was a vote for Finland, but Senator Bailey of North Carolina observed that a vote for the Brown Bill could mean almost anything.

> If anyone in Arizona complains to him that he voted for a loan to Finland, he can say, "Oh no, I did not vote for a loan to Finland. I voted to give the Export-Import Bank some money. I did not think about any loan to Finland." If there should be some Bolshevik in that state—of course, I do not think there is—who would complain to him, he could say, "Why, I have not offended you. I did not vote anything for Finland." But if on the next day, he should meet some friends of Finland—some men who have been greatly stirred by the gallantry of that little nation, standing there and fighting for her life—he might say, "I understood you said yesterday that

> you did not vote any loan to Finland. I am going to vote against you." The Senator would say, "Oh yes, I did. I voted for Finland because I was assured by Mr. Jesse Jones that that was exactly what he was going to do with the money.[6]

Jones, Chairman of the R.F.C., became one of the most important Administration spokesmen during this period primarily because no one seemed to know what to do. Roosevelt, in a letter to Speaker of the House Bankhead and Vice-President Garner, wrote that "the facts in regard to Finland are just as fully in the possession of every member of Congress as they are in the Executive Branch of the Government" and refused to go further than observe that something like the Brown Bill would be the "most reasonable approach."[7] When asked whether he supported the bill, however, F.D.R. dodged the question neatly. Hull, true to the course set on the outset of World War II, also refused to intervene with his congressional friends.[8] It was only through this thoroughly un-Rooseveltian abdication of control that a secondary figure such as Jones could be thrust into the spotlight.

The first important test of the Brown Bill came in the Senate Foreign Relations Committee, where it met with opposition from two camps. On the one hand, Senator Harrison stressed the argument that the money could better be used in aiding Americans than Europeans. Hiram Johnson claimed that the loan would violate the letter and spirit of neutrality. Harrison and Johnson shared the leadership in the Senate debates during the consideration of the Brown Bill. The former found himself in a position which would enable him to repay Roosevelt for having aided in replacing him as Senate Majority

Leader. As Chairman of the Finance Committee he was prepared to block the bill should it be reported there; as ranking member of the Foreign Relations Committee he was in another key position. Harrison argued that if he helped Finland, he could not face the voters back home who were suffering from agricultural depressions and sorely needed federal aid. He added that the Finnish loan would mean an increase in taxes, and he strongly opposed raising the federal debt limit as well. Harrison spent half the time arguing for more government spending for farmers, the other half demanding that federal "giveaways" be ended. In the heat of the debate, these inconsistencies went unnoticed.[9]

When Johnson rose to examine Jones, the emphasis shifted to the international implications of the bill. "We are all sympathetic to Finland," he declared, thus aligning himself on the side of the angels. "We are all anxious to see Finland 'whip the tar' out of Russia." To Johnson, however, American interests came first. "We are more sympathetic to our country than with any other. We do not want to do anything which may under any circumstances involve this country in war." He then asked: "You have that opinion, do you not?" Jones could but meekly respond, "I have."[10]

Speaking for the Administration, Jones argued that as he interpreted the Brown Bill the loan could not be used to finance the Finnish war effort and could not be considered a violation of neutrality. Within a period of less than five minutes he gave three assurances to Johnson that the R.F.C. would not even consider a military loan.[11] Indeed, so intent was the Administrator in denying the value of the loan that White of Maine indicated his belief that the Brown Bill merely represented an attempt on the part of the Administration to lend money around the world, and not a measure which would aid the Finns.[12] Jones was forced to defend a bill which ostensibly was for Finnish aid, and at the same time deny the efficacy of that aid. He had a difficult time of it. Spotlighted as he was, with radio commentators and newspapermen anxious for his every word, he could do little but temporize, thus clouding the issues more than before.

Nevertheless, the Brown Bill was reported out of Committee by a vote of twelve to six. Most of the Democrats voted for the measure, which was carried with the aid of La Follette, Shipstead and Vandenberg from the Scandinavian-American midwest. Johnson reluctantly voted for the measure, warning as he did that he would not stand for any expansion of the program which might make the United States a "wet nurse to the world."[13] Harrison, Van Nuys, George, Reynolds, Clark and Capper voted against the Brown Bill. All were either long-time isolationists, non-interventionists, or bitter foes of of the Administration.

On February 8 the Brown Bill was placed before the Senate. In an attempt to thwart the bill's supporters, Harrison also introduced a measure which would memorialize the Securities and Exchange Commisssion to aid the Finnish Government in floating a private issue in the United States, thus removing direct Government intervention in the matter.[14] Pro-Finnish senators demonstrated that the proposal was meaningless, since the S.E.C. did not need such a bill to help float the issue. Harrison was forced to admit that his measure might "not result in any material assistance to Finland," but was merely an "effort in the right direction." Harrison's attempt to substitute this avowal of good will for the Brown Bill was defeated by a vote of sixty-three to three.[15]

With this out of the way, discussion on the Brown Bill began. The arguments of the Committee were repeated as from February 8 to the 14th the senators took turns condemning the U.S.S.R. and praising Finland. Wiley called the Soviet leaders "international rapists" and McKeller inveighed against "the cowardly, dastardly, and miserable fight which Russia is making on Finland."[16] Little light was shed on what the Brown Bill actually meant. It was for Finland and against the U.S.S.R., and that was all most senators cared to know about it. McCarren announced that he would support "any measure that would aid Finland in its present struggle" but he would not vote for the bill because it would involve the United States in European affairs.[17] This, despite the fact that the Brown Bill merely authorized the R.F.C. to lend the money to Finland for non-military uses, and that the Finns had not yet exhausted previous credits for this purpose, an important fact mentioned by Jones but ignored by the press and the Senate.[18] Capper and George defended their Committee votes by insisting on several occasions that they were "strong for Finland," but that Americans needed aid more than foreigners.[19] Lundeen of Minnesota, with a large Scandinavian-American element watching his words, introduced into the record the story of a woman who was forced to give away her sons because she could not provide food for them on her husband's $15 a week paycheck. As long as conditions such as this prevailed, said Lundeen, he would not support foreign aid.[20]

The debate ended on February 13, when the Senate vote took place.[21] The delicacy of the issue was reflected in the fact that twenty of the senators voted in pairs rather than on the Senate floor. In all, fifty-eight voted for the measure with twenty-nine against. That almost a third of the upper house had voted against Finland was indicative of the strong non-interventionist sentiment in that body. The measure next went to the House, where hearings before the Committee on Banking and Currency began on February 16. As the Representatives began their deliberations, fresh Soviet gains on all fronts were reported.

The House investigations were dull and unimaginative. The measure passed the Committee by a vote of eighteen to five, the only change from the Senate version being a provision to allow Finland to purchase commercial aircraft with the funds gained from any American loan.

The Representatives began their discussions of the Brown Bill on February 21, but the cumbersome lower house delayed full scale debate until the 27th. The Representatives, closer to the grass-roots than their colleagues in the Senate, reflected public attitudes more accurately. In addition, those with Scandinavian-American constituents were more violent than their counterparts in the upper house. The eastern interventionists and internationalists were also more vocal. Celler of New York asked for an arms bill for Finland.[22] Dingall protested that the Brown Bill restricted purchases to "powder puffs, silken scanty pants and creampuffs when we know the Finns need shrapnel, buckshot, barbed wire and all the fiercest implements of hell because they are fighting to stop the Antichrist and the hosts of Hell."[23] Even arch-isolationist Hamilton Fish jumped on the bandwagon, introducing a bill to raise the capitalization of the Bank with the proviso that the additional funds be loaned to Finland. The New Yorker was taking no chances on a possible credit to the Allies.[24]

The House non-interventionists were as vocal as the interventionists. Representatives Rankin and Sumner warned that Finnish aid was the first step to actual military intervention, and Vorys suggested that the only safe way to help Finland was to contribute to the Hoover Fund.[25] Despite their speeches against the measure, the House non-interventionists were cognizant of the popularity of Finnish aid. They insisted on not having a roll call on the measure and, although the Brown Bill was accepted by a vote of 168-51, the public never knew who voted for and against it.[26] When the congressional leaders of both houses met to iron out differences in the two versions, the provision for the sale of commercial aircraft to Finland—the only provision which might have aided that nation militarily—was dropped. The bill went to the White House on March 2, and was signed immediately by F.D.R. On the same day Jesse Jones announced that the non-military loan to Finland had been approved by the R.F.C., and both the Administration and Congress turned to other business.[27]

The Brown Bill probably reflected the sentiments of most Americans. It represented the halfway house between interventionism and non-interventionism. Interventionists could applaud its passage as a sign of American willingness to participate in a limited way in the European conflict; the non-interventionist could justifiably observe that it also signified a determination to remain aloof militarily.

The congressional debates also indicated a new public awareness of foreign affairs. The question of Finnish aid was not stated in economic, geographic or military terms; if it were, the non-interventionists would have been able to present a stronger case. Instead, the Finnish cause was portrayed almost entirely in terms of emotionalism and basic ideology. It was possible to argue against aid to the Allies on the basis of the World War I experience and by appealing to the strong strain of Anglophobia present in many areas of the nation. But the American people had every reason to like Finland and to dislike her adversary. Many Americans demanded action, and the Brown Bill seemed to be the answer to their cries for aid to Finland. The vote on this measure may be considered the first positive step Congress had taken in behalf of a belligerent since 1919. The Brown Bill represented direct aid—a new departure—while the legislation of the previous months was indirect.

At the same time, the Brown Bill's vagueness and restrictions were such that its impact on the War was nil. Perhaps the best indication of this was Ambassador Oumansky's reaction to its passage. The Soviet representative had complained on many occasions about the moral embargo, but he never raised the issue of the Brown Bill and the R.F.C. loans. He knew that the American people harbored ill feelings toward his nation, but he also knew that the American government had no intention of disrupting Soviet-American relations any more than was absolutely necessary. The loans were little more than pious expressions of sympathy, but in the light of American opinion at the time, little more could have been expected. The *Milwaukee Journal,* which throughout the War took a starkly realistic view of the situation, called the loans "empty gestures."

> Everybody . . . knows what we are preparing to do is fling a sop to Finland. We do not want to go to war. Nor do we want to turn our backs entirely on Finland. So we will give her money in a form that Russia cannot legitimately object to; and that will not help Finland unless some other country will do the "dirty work" of translating our non-military loan into military aid through an exchange of goods.[28]

NOTES

Chapter VII: CONGRESSIONAL ACTION

1 The best statistical data on this subject can be found in Cantril, *Public Opinion,* p. 1101 ff.

2 Roosevelt admitted that "there is without a doubt in the United States a great desire for some action to assist Finland," but at the same time added that "there is . . . undoubted opposition to the creation of precedents which might lead to large credits to nations in Europe, whether belligerents or neutrals." F.D.R. closed by stating that Congress had as much information as his office, and could act as it saw fit. Original draft in *Roosevelt Papers.* Also, *New York Times,* January 17, 1940.

3 Celler's bill would have allowed the Finns to purchase American anti-aircraft guns, while Dingall's would authorize the sale of Garand rifles to Finland, before the American Army received them! *New York Times,* December 24, 1939; January 11, 1940.

4 United States Senate, *Hearings Before the Committee on Foreign Relations,* 76th Congress, 3rd Session, on S. 3069 (Washington, 1940); *New York Times,* January 10, 1940.

5 *Congressional Record,* February 13, 1940, p. 1384.

6 *Ibid.,* February 9, 1940, p. 1279.

7 *New York Times,* January 17, 1940.

8 Hull, *Memoirs,* I, 741; Langer and Gleason, *Challenge to Isolation,* 339; *Moffat Papers,* p. 290.

9 Foreign Relations Committee, *Hearings on S. 3069,* p. 3 ff.; *New York Times,* January 31, 1940.

10 *Ibid.,* pp. 27-28.

11 *Ibid.,* pp. 18-19.

12 *Ibid.,* pp. 28-29.

13 *New York Times,* February 8, 1940.

14 *Congressional Record,* February 8, 1940, pp. 1223-24. At the time Republic of Finland bonds were at 45 with no takers. *Wall Street Journal,* February 9, 1940.

15 *Congressional Record,* February 9, 1940, p. 1225.

16 *Ibid.,* p. 1229.

17 *Ibid.,* p. 1276; *New York Times,* February 10, 1940.
ruary 10, 1940.

18 United States House of Representatives, *Hearings Before the Committee on Banking and Currency on S. 3069 (H.R. 8477), A Bill to Provide for Increasing the Lending Authority of the Export-Import Bank of Washington and for other Purposes* (Washington, 1940), pp. 4, 33-34.

19 *Congressional Record,* February 13, 1940, p. 1389.

20 *Washington Daily News,* February 8, 1940, as cited in *Ibid.,* February 13, 1940, p. 1399.

21 *Ibid.,* February 13, 1940, p. 1405. For the end of the debate, see Denys Smith, *America and the Axis War* (London, 1942), pp. 214-15.

22 *New York Times,* February 23, 1940; *Congressional Record,* February 15, 1940, pp. 1518-19.

23 *Life* (Vol. 8, No. 11, March 11, 1940), p. 28.

24 *New York Times,* February 28, 1940.

25 *Congressional Record,* February 27, 1940, p. 2040; February 28, 1940, pp. 2102, 2110.

26 *Ibid.,* February 27, 1940, p. 2110.

27 *New York World Telegram,* March 2, 1940.

28 *Milwaukee Journal,* February 17, 1940.

Chapter VIII

THE MEANING OF THE CONGRESSIONAL VOTE

As has been observed, Finland did not receive significant aid as a result of the passage of the Brown Bill. Indeed, this innocuous piece of legislation was far more important for the United States than for either adversary in the Winter War, for it marked the first attempt on the part of the nation to intervene directly in the European conflicts.

Up to that time the Government had confined its role to indirect actions. Although the enactment of cash-and-carry and arms embargo repeal had aided the Allies greatly, many congressmen tried to defend these bills as an attempt to return to freedom of the seas; they were acts of internationalism, but not of interventionism. In addition, the legislation pertained to private corporations. Congress and the President carefully refrained from taking a stand in behalf of England and France. There were speeches and public statements, but no action.

The Finnish loan, on the other hand, was a positive move which directly involved a governmental agency in a foreign war. By granting a loan to Finland the nation was not attempting to defend an impersonal legal right such as freedom of the seas; it was aiding one nation and, by inference, harming another. Slight and feeble though it was, the loan was the first attempt on the part of the United States to take a positive stand toward the wars. The more prescient journals noted this and observed that it marked a new direction in American foreign policy, one which could lead to embarrassing complications. "We are far from criticizing these steps" wrote the *Nation*, "but it is well to realize that they lead in a direction quite contrary to the Neutrality Act."

> At present the Allies are not at war with Russia, but they are sending Finland what aid they can, and if the war spreads to Scandinavia they may well decide on open intervention, merging the two wars now in progress in Europe into one. We should then have to drop financial aid to the Finns, insisting on cash-and-carry, or find ourselves in a very illogical tangle.[1]

One of the better ways to understand how the nation got itself into this position is to study the Senate during the discussions pertaining to repeal of the arms embargo, and the Finnish Aid debate.

Forty-six senators voted both for repeal of the arms embargo and passage of the Brown Bill, indicating a willingness to enter European affairs on both counts. Southern Democrats, in the forefront during the fight for embargo repeal, were equally active during the Finnish loan debates. Without the support of sixteen southerners neither bill would have passed. Their impact was great, due to their unanimity and their dominance of the congressional debates on the measures. Tennessee's McKeller declared that he would vote for embargo repeal "because it operates to injure two of the great democracies of the world, England and France." Andrews of Florida asserted that "Hitler and Stalin stand for governmental and social conditions which we must abhor, while England and France stand for the things we even hold dearer than life itself, and know to be essential to the peace and liberty of man."[2] Bailey of North Carolina, a rabid isolationist who in the past had voiced fears of "meddling in European affairs," voted for both measures grudgingly.[3] The South was historically the home of American internationalism, and in 1939-1940 southern senators spearheaded the drive for interventionism.

Eleven Democrats and eight Republicans from the North also voted for both measures. Support for interventionism transcended party lines in this section alone. Internationalists like Vermont's Warren Austin and Maine's Hale, both Republicans, spoke out against the Soviets throughout the War. New Jersey's Barbour, who was uninterested in foreign affairs before the conflicts, suggested breaking diplomatic relations with the Soviet Union and became a staunch interventionist during the War.[4] Democrats Maloney of Connecticut and Tydings of Maryland stated that positive steps against Stalin would do more to prevent war than any other action, and urged that America lead a crusade against the Soviets.[5]

All seven of the midwesterners who voted for both measures were Democrats, but indications are that some voted out of party loyalty rather than any strong convictions in the field of foreign policy. Brown was silent during the special session. Truman and Illinois' Lucas and Slattery declared in favor of the Brown Bill but absented themselves from the final roll calls. Lucas was the only one of the three to speak on either measure; he defended his arms embargo vote by saying that it did not mean that he held a brief "for imperialistic England or imperialistic France.[6] The only midwesterner who tried to defend either internationalism or interventionism was Burke of Nebraska, who argued that the Neutrality

Act in practice was prejudicial to the Allies, and therefore should be repealed in the name of true neutralism.[7]

The nine senators from the Far West were also all Democrats who apparently voted for the measures out of party loyalty or some beliefs which they kept to theirselves. Their leader, Key Pittman of the Foreign Relations Committee, was conspicuous by his absence from both debates.

This internationalist-interventionist group—almost half the Senate—was to control that body during the years ahead. The New Deal coalition of Southern Democrats, minorities, and intellectuals, was to give way to a faction which believed that the nation must play a more important role in foreign affairs than it had in the past. Some were old time internationalists who took a legalistic view toward American involvement; others were primarily interested in catering to hyphenate Americans. Some, like Florida's Claude Pepper, were Roosevelt men who voted the straight F.D.R. ticket without much in the way of independent thought. Others, most notably Harry Truman, would stumble into the coalition and through it find world importance. But in 1939-1940 the coalition was held together by expedients, emotionalism, and the hope that the public would support its stand.

A far smaller group stood against them on both issues, men who comprised the core of the isolationist and non-interventionist movements. In all fourteen senators, by their actions during the two votes, declared against involvement.

Three came from the North. Two were Republicans and one a Democrat. Danaher of Connecticut and Massachusett's Lodge, the Republicans, were silent during the debate on the Brown Bill, but the former was active during the special session. The Democrat, Holt of West Virginia, was a strong Anglophobe who launched bitter attacks against those who supported embargo repeal.[8] It is significant that Holt had announced his intention to retire in 1940 while neither Danaher nor Lodge would be up for re-election in that year.

Only one southerner—Reynolds of South Carolina—voted against both measures. One of the loudest and vilest demagogues ever to sit in the Senate, he inserted several near-purple passages in the *Congressional Record.*[9] Affiliated as he was with almost all the important "hate groups" of the time, Reynolds was viewed with embarrassment by those who came to the same conclusions as he but for different reasons.

Six midwesterners voted against both measures, three of whom were Democrats, two Republicans, and one Farmer-Laborite. Of the Democrats, only Clark spoke in both debates. He asked the nation to remain aloof from "the old, old, age-long quarrels of Europe."[10] South Dakota's Bulow, more of a pacifist than an isolationist, declared that he would "rather take a chance on Hitler's word than . . . on sacrificing a million American boys for the pleasure of hanging Mr. Hitler on any kind of a tree."[11] Republican Capper of Kansas was an irreconcilable isolationist who announced his intention "to vote against every proposal which I believe would tend toward involving us in that war."[12] Wisconsin's Wiley strongly opposed meddling in European affairs, calling the Brown Bill "an overt act in violation of international law and the Constitution."[13] Farmer-Laborite Ernest Lundeen of Minnesota was the most rabid isolationist in the Senate, delivering biting attacks on "international meddlers" and "world savers" on several occasions during both debates.[14] With Clark and Reynolds he conducted a serious discussion on how, at some future date, the United States could seize Canada. Any aid to Great Britain, he said, should be predicated on that nation's surrender of her colonies to the United States.[15] "Let's seize Bermuda" was his rejoinder to another senator's question as to how the nation should act if Britain were defeated.[16]

Two of the four Far Western senators who voted in the same way were more interested in internal affairs than in foreign policy, Johnson and Borah both voted against embargo repeal, and the Californian teamed with Borah's successor, Thomas, in opposition to the Brown Bill.

Those who voted against both bills comprised a far less distinguished group than those on the other side of the issues. With the exception of Johnson and, for a while, Borah, they lacked leadership and national prestige. As the nation moved in the direction of interventionism, these men would either be cast aside, as would be the case with Clark, or would convert to the other camp, as did Lodge. The failure of this irreconcilable band to command a larger following in the Senate or the nation was testimony to the lack of vitality on the part of their brand of isolationism in early 1940.

The most important senators in terms of influence were those whose votes were different on the two votes. Without them the interventionists would have lacked a majority and could not have forged a new foreign policy for the nation. These were the men who saw a difference between internationalism and interventionism, who accepted one and rejected the other. More than the others they seemed to recognize the problems facing American foreign policy in 1939-1940. Next to the southerners they were the most vocal group, and in their words can be seen the best reflection of the Great Debate of the time.

Of those senators who either voted for repeal of the arms embargo or abstained on the roll call, fifteen opposed the Brown Bill. All but three were from the South and Midwest, and the group included such important old leaders as George and Harrison and new ones like Robert Taft.

Many of those who voted in this fashion argued that their opposition to the arms embargo represented a desire to act absolutely neutral in the European wars. These senators believed that there was no inconsistency between internationalism and neutralism. Indeed, the only true neutralism lay in a willingness to treat all belligerents alike without sacrificing such basic rights as freedom of the seas. This position, which may be described as neo-Wilsonian after that President's 1914 stand, was adopted by such old Wilsonians as Texas' Tom Connally, who led the attack on Nye when the Munitions Committee began to probe too deeply into American foreign policy during World War I. The same may be said of Harrison, who, in his hatred of F.D.R., never abandoned the internationalist stance he had taken decades earlier. In opposing the Brown Bill the Mississippian carefully stated his desire for more New Deal measures *rather than* aid to Finland, in contradistinction to Capper, who supported the New Deal and *opposed* Finnish aid. This was the basic difference between those internationalists who voted against the Brown Bill and the isolationists who acted in the same fashion.

An interesting case in point is that of Robert Taft, who has been unjustly condemned (and praised) as the great defender of isolationism. In reality, Taft was one of the few G.O.P. leaders who was willing to come out against the embargo. Unlike Vandenberg, Nye and Clark, he never closed his eyes to European events, and unlike Johnson and Borah he did not view all European nations with fear and hatred. In 1939-1940 he was most sympathetic to the Allied cause, and in 1941 he was to say that "a victory for Communism would be far more dangerous to the United States than a victory for Fascism." [17] Taft voted for embargo repeal feeling that by so acting he was placing the United States "in a stronger position to resist all possible involvement in Europe." But Taft was not a true interventionist, and would die opposing that doctrine. He claimed that "no sensible British or French observer will advise his government that the passage of this law is any symbol of an American desire to enter the European War." [18]

The eighteen senators who voted for the Brown Bill or abstained from the roll after voting against embargo repeal were the new interventionists, men who would commit the nation to act in specific foreign situations but would, in general, deny that America need abandon isolationism in "normal times." This was just the opposite of the internationalist view of men like Hull, which was that the nation should play a world role in times of calm, but must refrain from taking sides in foreign wars. Massachusetts' Senator Walsh, an Anglophobe, told reporters that "if embargo repeal is neutrality, then

God save America!"[19] Walsh argued that the new World War was one for "the furtherance of nationalistic interests, and the preservation of the European balance of power." "This is not a war for the ideals of democracy," he said, and the United States had nothing to gain by aiding either side.[20] On the other hand, Walsh was willing to aid the Finns and voted for the Brown Bill.

Five of the interventionists came from the Midwest. Even when the pressure of large Scandinavian- and German-American constituencies in this part of the country are taken into account, the votes of these five—Vandenberg, Nye, Shipstead, La Follette, and Frazier—are most significant in the turn to interventionism. All were important either nationally or sectionally. Vandenberg was an avowed candidate for the presidency and, when that bid failed, had to stand for re-election to the Senate. In 1939-1940 his was the clearest and sanest isolationist voice in the Senate. Vandenberg's moderation and at the same time devotion to the doctrine made him the natural leader of the isolationists. "Our status today must be of scrupulous detachment," he said.[21] A stand of this nature would endear him to Michigan isolationists, but what of the nation as a whole? Vandenberg hoped for national office, and realized that such a position would be unpopular in the East. As an isolationist, he voted against embargo repeal, but as a politician, he was for the Brown Bill. This was to be his only interventionist or internationalist act before America entered the war in 1941. Interestingly enough, the other senatorial presidential hopeful, Taft, voted against Vandenberg on both occasions. Taft's position was entirely logical, while Vandenberg's action cannot be explained in any other way than as being an act of expediency. It was, however, an important milestone in his life and may be looked upon as the first step along the road which eventually would make him the G.O.P. interventionist spokesman in the Senate.

Frazier of North Dakota also fought the arms embargo repeal as the only way to remain truly neutral.[22] La Follette agreed, considering repeal as "a significant step toward participation in the European war." [23] But both were up for election in 1940 and felt that the Brown Bill had to be accepted in order to placate their Scandinavian-American constituencies.[24] Nye was in a similar situation, although he did not have to face the voters at that time. He strongly opposed embargo repeal, stating that should it pass, the United States would become "the silent partner of the British Empire." [25] When the Finnish loan discussions began, Nye told reporters that passage of the Brown Bill would be "a step toward war." "I hate some of these European situations," he explained, "but my hate is not strong enough to make me want to jeopardize our institutions as they would be jeopardized if we become involved in a war." [26] After this, letters of protest began to pour into his office from irate constituents. Within a week Nye was quoted as being "concerned" with the Finnish situation,[27] and he discreetly absented himself from the vote. In many ways, Nye's silence was as eloquent as Vandenberg's shift.

Six far western senators voted for the Brown Bill after opposing arms embargo repeal. One was Oregon's McNary, a G.O.P. leader of national stature. His nomination for the vice-presidency was evidence of his ability to please those party conservatives who considered Willkie a Republican version of F.D.R. and who demanded McNary to balance the ticket. Idaho's Clark voted in the same manner. In speaking against arms embargo repeal, he stated that such an action would undoubtedly aid Great Britain and France to crush Germany. The dislocation following Hitler's defeat would cause "an Empire of Communism" to rise in central Europe "which would be a threat to the peace and safety of the world."[28] Dislike for Communism was as important as sympathy for Finland in the minds and hearts of most of the interventionists. Clark probably did not foresee that he and those who thought like him would form the majority leadership in the Senate a generation later.

NOTES

Chapter VIII: THE MEANING OF THE CONGRESSIONAL VOTE

1 *Nation* (Vol. 149, No. 27, December 30, 1939), p. 723.

2 *Congressional Record,* 76th Congress, 2nd Session, October 20, 1939; October 21, p. 682.

3 *Ibid.,* October 10, 1939, pp. 244-47.

4 *Ibid.,* October 10, 1939, p. 232; October 11, 1939, p. 267; October 17, 1939, pp. 400, 501; *New York Times,* December 9, 1939.

5 *Ibid.,* October 10, 1939, p. 232; October 17, 1939, p. 501.

6 *Ibid.,* October 17, 1939, p. 512.

7 *Ibid.,* October 20, 1939, p. 643.

8 *Ibid.,* October 18, 1939, p. 546.

9 *Ibid.,* October 12, 1939, p. 312.

10 *Ibid.,* October 11, 1939, p. 268.

11 *Ibid.,* October 12, 1939, p. 312.

12 *Ibid.,* October 8, 1939, p. 45.

13 *Ibid.,* January 8, 1940, p. 101.

14 *Ibid.,* October 12, 1939, p. 312.

15 *Ibid.,* October 12, 1939, pp. 347-51.

16 *Time* (Vol. 35, No. 10, March 4, 1940), p. 13.

17 Forrest Davis and Ernest K. Lindley, *How War Came* (New York, 1942), p. 243.

18 *Congressional Record,* October 13, 1939, pp. 355-60.

19 *New York Times,* October 12, 1939.

20 *Congressional Record,* October 17, 1939, p. 497.

21 *Ibid.,* October 4, 1939, pp. 95-104.

22 *Ibid.,* October 14, 1939, p. 397.

23 *Ibid.,* October 12, 1939, p. 321.

24 Of those senators up for re-election, 25 voted for the Brown Bill, 8 against, and one was registered as not voting.

25 *Congressional Record,* October 13, 1939, p. 360.

26 *New York Times,* January 11, 1940.

27 A.A. Berle in *Ibid.,* January 14, 1940.

28 *Congressional Record,* October 16, 1939, p. 446; *New York Times,* March 1, 1940.

Chapter IX

INTERVENTIONISM AND NATIONAL POLITICS

The Winter War took place during the presidential campaign of 1939-1940, and played a brief role in the electioneering of the hopefuls. All candidates considered the U.S.S.R. to be the villain in the piece, and each major party tried to outdo the other in castigating Stalin, the Red Army, and Communism in general, to the obvious delight of the electorate. This was a sharp reversal of the public attitude of early 1939, when a poll indicated that the American people would have favored the U.S.S.R. in a war against Germany by the margin of more than four to one. During the Winter War the public indicated that it was more strongly against Stalin in his war then against Hitler in the greater conflict.[1] This sentiment led many to believe that American intervention in one or perhaps both wars was not long in coming. "There is a hot wind beginning to rustle in the parched grasses among our best people, a wind that may in time start a prairie fire in eagerness to fight Hitler and Stalin."[2]

This combination of war fever and interventionism affected both parties. Most Republican leaders endorsed Roosevelt's position, though a few of the more honest ones professed that so far as they could see, the Government had studiously avoided taking any position at all. By and large the moderate members of the opposition were "finding it easier to accept what they have been induced to consider the inevitable."[3] But a political party does not win elections by merely endorsing opposition views. The public reaction to the Winter War and the Administration's inability to find a clear cut policy toward the conflict gave some Republicans a much needed issue to use against the President.

The Republican National Committee acted within days of the Soviet attack. On December 4 it made public the statements of several prominent Republicans who had opposed recognition of the U.S.S.R. in 1933.[4] Apparently the Committee was attempting to embarrass the Administration with its left wing supporters; by standing convicted of an overfriendly attitude toward Stalinism the Democratic Party would face a difficult time at the polls. Minnesota's Representative Knudson, an isolationist who favored the Brown Bill, charged that "no offer of good offices or pious expressions of sympathy will enable the Roosevelt Administration to escape its share of responsibility for the tragedy that has overtaken Finland." By recognizing the Soviets, F.D.R. had "immeasurably strengthened the hand of the dictator Stalin." [5] In directing this blast, Knudson echoed the views of several G.O.P. interventionists.[6]

This faction's attempt to sever relations with the U.S.S.R. was soon carried into the field of presidential politics. One observer noted that Vandenberg was more isolationist than Taft, and that Dewey had not made his position clear.[7] The last, an unknown quantity and quality, announced his candidacy on November 31, the day of the Soviet attack. He set up offices in all major cities and personally directed the activities of a well-oiled machine.[8] Dewey hoped to get the nomination without making many commitments, especially in the foreign policy area. Always an astute politician, he knew that his position made such a plan feasible. Taft and Vandenberg were in the midst of senatorial battles and could not avoid taking stands, thus alienating potential supporters. Dewey, who held no national office, could easily play the role of critic without offering positive programs. Since all abhorred the Soviets, he was safe in stating that "the Godless government has raised up to a state creed the sterile doctrine of atheism. It has achieved power by the annual murder of large numbers of its own people."[9] Dewey castigated Roosevelt for recognizing the U.S.S.R. and expressed the hope that he would "stop trying to make deals with Russia."[10] Although he did not make clear his own program for dealing with the Soviets, Dewey did not turn to isolationism at any time during the campaign. Basically an opportunist, he realized that the nation swiftly was becoming interventionist and he attempted to reflect this switch. At an important New York rally, he said:

> We in America cannot escape being affected by these tragedies. Nor can we remain unmoved by the agony through which millions of men, women, and little children are passing daily, both in Europe and in Asia. For their sakes—for our own sake—We must search for the moment when we might, without entanglement, use our good offices to effect a genuine peace.[11]

These are hardly the words of an interventionist, but the isolationists could take little comfort from them.

Robert Taft was far more straightforward during the campaign. A few days after the Soviet attack he told reporters that "the greatest issue of the 1940 campaign will be keeping America out of war." The G.O.P., he believed, must be considered the peace party in such a campaign.[12] But Taft did not attack the Roosevelt leadership at this time. He hoped that a bi-partisan foreign policy might be adopted, and he voted for repeal of the arms embargo in this hope. Taft tried to campaign on domestic issues instead. He attacked the New Deal as being destructive of individualism and ask for a balanced budget and less spending. At first he avoided foreign affairs completely, at one time going so far as to declare that there was no difference between the Democrats and Republicans on the question of adequate preparation for defense. Statements such as this won Taft the applause of John Foster Dulles, who almost left the Dewey camp for the Ohioan at this time, and the opprobrium of Borah, who spoke for the isolationists.[13]

Nevertheless, as the campaign wore on Taft began to speak out more clearly on foreign policy, specifically to criticize F.D.R. for implying "that we have some duty to interfere abroad." He echoed the old cry that "entrance into the European War would be a greater threat to American democracy than to the dictatorships of Europe."[14] Taft sympathized with the Allies, but stated that "because we sympathize with one side is no reason why we should run onto the field and try to play in the game." Despite this, the Ohio senator added that "Finland presents a special case. . . . We certainly owe something to the Finnish people."[15] This was said, however, after the War.

If Dewey spoke for the undecided and Taft for the non-interventionists, Vandenberg reflected the views of midwestern isolationists. Nye began to campaign for his

Munitions Investigations colleague early in January, calling Vandenberg the nation's single best hope for peace. But how would he deal with the European wars? Vandenberg was in no position to take a stand. He could not temporize, for he had to take a stance in the Senate. He could not accept interventionism, for if he did, he would lose his midwestern supporters. Nor could Vandenberg ignore the European wars without leaving himself open to accusations of not being a realist. As a result, the Senator was unable to present a coherent program. He refused to campaign, but at the same time also refused to drop out of the race. The spectacle of the leader of the senatorial isolationists facing these quandries in this clumsy fashion reflected the confusion of his followers. Vandenberg did not have a chance unless a strong reaction against the Roosevelt foreign policy developed between January and convention time, and it was evident that no such development would take place.[16]

These were the three leading aspirants for the Republican presidential nomination. Each had been either isolationist or non-interventionist prior to the European wars, and all had to adjust their positions as a result of these wars. During the campaign Dewey would remain the trimmer, Taft would remain non-interventionist, and Vandenberg would remain intransigent. But all three were forced to take note of the European wars, and all were obliged to consider means of meeting the challenge of war. The Republican Party was moving away from isolationism, and the eventual nomination of Wendell Willkie marked that doctrine's demise in the G.O.P. Willkie represented the coming to political power of a new factor—of a group which did not feel obliged to defend the Johnson Act, the Neutrality Acts, or the Munitions Investigations. Willkie looked to the future rather than to the past. He hadn't the moral obligation to defend isolationism as had Vandenberg, or the political past of Dewey or Taft. More than any other presidential hopeful he was uncommitted and could view the foreign policy scene without the ideological difficulties which plagued men like Vandenberg. Indeed, there was little to choose between Willkie and Roosevelt in the sphere of foreign relations. By election day, the spirit of bipartisanship had taken root. Although more than a year would pass before it would flourish, the Great Debate was over before 1941.

Isolationism remained strong in some quarters, however. Those who favored non-entanglement and could not stomach Vandenberg's vacillations turned to Frank Gannett, a wealthy and influential publisher who campaigned for what amounted to a return to the Coolidge era of free enterprise and the Nye era of fear and distrust of foreigners. He agreed that Finland deserved American sympathy, but considered all aid proposals to be out of the question. "If we should begin to lend money to Finland where would it stop?" The lending of money got the nation into war in 1917, and Gannett opposed all steps which seemed to lead in the same direction.[17] But men like Gannett, and later on Hoover, who was also mentioned as a presidential possibility, were not taken seriously by the party or the nation. The public would no longer accept the isolationist formulas. Failing in attempts to synthesize a new policy, the Republicans were forced to accept the Roosevelt program in the nomination of Willkie.

The Democrats were in a better position than the Republicans, although F.D.R.'s third term ambitions and his foreign policy shifts strained the coalition somewhat. A group of conservative southerners began to support Vice-President Garner at this time, hoping to use him to head off a third term and foreign involvement.[18] Were it not for the skilful machinations of Sam Rayburn, a serious southern defection might have taken place.[19] At the same time, Irish Catholic spokesmen began to attack the President for his pro-British statements. This was balanced in part by the support Roosevelt's policies received from Al Smith and others, but important elements of the Catholic press began a concerted attack on F.D.R. *Commonweal,* which consistently supported isolationism during the early part of the War, called upon all Americans to oppose any attempts to involve the United States in foreign conflicts. Lindbergh's sometime scurrilous attacks on the President were applauded as "rarely equalled in public circles for economy of phrase, mastery of expression, logic of development." *Commonweal* characterized the interventionists as "those die-hards of eighteenth century rationalism."[20] The rightest *Tablet* declared it would not succumb to the "war mongers," and campaigned for the retention of the arms embargo.[21] Father Coughlin, spokesman for the extreme right, denounced the "land grabbing, treaty-breaking imperialistic capitalism of the English and French governments" and called for an end of cooperation with them.[22]

Catholic isolationism existed side by side with a bitter hatred of the Soviet Union. Both the *Tablet* and *Commonweal* devoted editorials to the religious persecutions in the U.S.S.R., and one gets the impression that both organs would have welcomed a rupture with the Soviets. Coughlin was more vitriolic. In referring to the Nazi-Soviet attack on Poland he said *"This is Stalin's War. This is the Communist War. This is the Anti-Christ's War."* [23]

Being both isolationist and anti-Soviet, these Catholic publications were confused by the Winter War. In effect, they were forced to choose between isolationism as a doctrine or aid to Finland as an expedient. *Commonweal* and the *Tablet* chose the former. On December 15 *Commonweal* published its first comment on the War. In a carefully worded editorial the publication bent over backwards to see the Soviet point of view. Moscow attacked Finland in defense of the Soviet "conception of national sovereignty." Although the periodical concluded by stating that "one cannot see any excuse whatever for the Russian adventure" its tone was far milder than that of any major publication.[24] When the War ended *Commonweal* made no mention of the harsh dictated peace, but instead called on Finland to make the most of her situation. "If they showed courage during the fighting, they will need it in greater measure even to attempt to rebuild their country." [25]

The *Tablet* and Father Coughlin were more vindictive, but they too had no desire to enter a war. "The people of the world stand aghast at the brutal invasion of Finland by the Soviet Union" read a *Tablet* editorial,[26] but during the War itself the newspaper rarely mentioned the fighting. While Polish relief was supported frequently, Finnish aid organizations were totally disregarded. When the peace treaty was made public, the editors merely affirmed that "American sympathy has been with the Finns from the start of the conflict." [27]

Father Coughlin used the War to solidify his position as a leader of the isolationist crusade. Declaring that the Soviet attack had "jarred the American people more vigorously than any single incident since the sinking of the Lusitania" he nevertheless would have Roosevelt take no other action than to withdraw recognition of the Moscow regime.[28] Although he personally donated $1,000 to the Hoover Fund, *Social Justice* was wary of the Brown Bill.[29] Coughlin did not seem to know what to do. He publicly endorsed the bill, but at the same time published a series of articles entitled "U.S. Neutrality Periled by Export-Import Bank" in *Social Justice*.[30]

These Catholic organs, torn as they were between noninterventionism and anti-Communism, reluctantly chose the former. Unlike other individuals and groups in a similar position, they did not accept interventionism at this time. Until the Japanese attack on Pearl Harbor the Catholic press vacillated, hesitated, and ignored the issues. Only then did these publications regain the vigor which marked them in the early 1930's. This confusion served to promote a status-quo mentality among the editors. Since they could not offer a positive program during the Winter War, they could afford to accept by default Roosevelt's weak stand. Due to the failure of Catholic leaders to head a moral crusade against the Administration's policies, that part of the New Deal coalition remained with the President.

Communists and fellow-travellers reacted in an opposite fashion. They had their moral crusade: support of the U.S.S.R. Because of Roosevelt's stand during the

Russo-Finnish War, many left the coalition. Others, followers of the *New Republic* which supported the United Front, confined their opposition to sharp criticism. "The American liberals who are busy snooting the Soviets ought to be warned that they are cooperating with some of the world's most powerful enemies of liberalism." [31] During the War *New Republic* charged that "the pro-Fascist leanings of many Finnish generals have been notorious." [32] In all, the magazine tried its best to absolve the U.S.S.R. of guilt and smear the Finns with a charge of pro-Fascism. Nevertheless, its editors continued to urge support of the President and was interventionist vis-à-vis the World War.

The American Youth Congress was split by the War. With Communists in important positions of power and a large national membership, its criticism of Roosevelt's Soviet policies were viewed with alarm by many new dealers. As soon as the War had begun, the leadership began its debate as to what position the A.Y.C. would take. Executive Secretary Joseph Lash led a group which sought to condemn the Soviets for their attack and ask the President for more aid to Finland. The dominant figure in the organization, Lash organized a New York meeting in January to discuss the question and have the organization take a stand. The left-wing faction retaliated by introducing a motion at the meeting to censure Finland for her pro-German leanings. Lash told his fellow delegates that a position against Finland would "divide all those who worked so hard to make a national American Youth Congress possible." [33] But Lash was in the minority. His motion to censure the Soviet Union was defeated by a vote of 322-49, and Lash was ousted as Executive Secretary and replaced by Herbert Witt, a nominee of the left-wing faction.[34]

Attempting to heal the rift and assure the New Deal of A.Y.C. support, Roosevelt addressed the Congress on February 10. Admitting that he himself had trusted the Soviets unduly, the President told the delegates that "the Soviet Union is run by a dictatorship as absolute as any other dictatorship in the world." These words evoked hissing and booing from the delegates, a rare sight for any president and especially rare for Roosevelt. The episode was indicative of the left-wingers' opposition to what to them appeared a new anti-Soviet tack in American foreign relations.[35] Their opposition was the only loss Roosevelt suffered as a result of the Russo-Finnish War.

Thus, while Republicans were attempting to find a new rationale, Democrats were able to close ranks after the initial shock of two European wars passed. With the exception of some extremists and those farmers who were dissatisfied with the Administration farm program, F.D.R. was still in control of those forces which had backed him in the landslide 1936 election. The people were moving toward interventionism, and Roosevelt was with them.

NOTES

Chapter IX: INTERVENTIONISM AND NATIONAL POLITICS

1 George Gallup in *New York Times,* January 1, 1940.

2 *New Republic* (Vol. 102, No. 7, February 12, 1940), pp. 198-99.

3 Arthur Krock in *New York Times,* January 21, 1940.

4 *Ibid.,* December 4, 1939.

5 *Ibid.,* December 3, 1939.

6 Speech by Representative Gore and comments by others in *Congressional Record,* February 27, 1940, p. 2065 ff.

7 Harold B. Hinton in *New York Times,* February 25, 1940.

8 *New York World Telegram,* December 1, 1939.

9 *Ibid.; New York Post,* January 20, 1940.

10 *New York Times,* January 20, 1940.

11 *Ibid.,* January 21, 1940.

12 *Ibid.,* December 3, 1939.

13 *Ibid.,* December 13, 1939.

14 *Ibid.,* January 20, 1940.

15 *Vital Speeches* (Vol. 6, No. 11, March 15, 1940), pp. 345-48.

16 Turner Catledge in *New York Times,* December 24, 1939; *New York World Telegram,* January 19, 1940.

17 *Ibid.,* January 24, 1940.

18 *New York Times,* January 18, 1940.

19 *Ibid.,* February 8, 1940.

20 *Commonweal* (Vol. 30, No. 23, September 29, 1939), p. 507; December 1, 1939, p. 102.

21 *Tablet,* September 23, 1939.

22 *Ibid., loc. cit.*

23 *Social Justice,* October 9, 1939.

24 *Commonweal* (Vol. 31, No. 8, December 15, 1939), p. 173.

25 *Ibid.* (Vol. 31, No. 22, March 22, 1940), p. 463.

26 *Tablet,* December 9, 1939.

27 *Ibid.,* March 23, 1940.

28 *Social Justice,* February 5, 1940.

29 *Christian Science Monitor,* December 4, 1939.

30 *Social Justice,* March 18, 1940.

31 *New Republic* (Vol. 101, No. 1302, November 15, 1939), p. 95.

32 *Ibid.* (Vol. 101, No. 1305, December 6, 1939), p. 179.

33 *New York Post,* January 3, 21, 1940; *New York Times,* February 4, 1940.

34 *New York Post,* February 5, 1940.

35 *New York Times,* February 11, 1940.

Chapter X

THE AFTERMATH

Peace negotiations between the Soviet Union and Finland were initiated during February of 1940. Finland was on the verge of defeat and the Soviet Union felt it imperative to liquidate her northern commitment and concentrate upon the more important threats from Japan and Germany.[1] Both nations had much to gain and little to lose by concluding a peace at that time. Despite attempts on the part of the Allies to aid the Finnish effort, Helsinki was ready to sign a Carthaginian peace.[2]

Roosevelt's contributions to the situation were slight, in keeping with the American attitude toward the War. On February 2, Ambassador Steinhardt saw Molotov and discussed the possibilities of peace. The Commissar denounced the Helsinki Government in strong language, and Steinhardt had to report that he "was unable to obtain from Molotov any clear statement as to the attitude of his Government to an approach from my Government."[3]

The United States took no further action until March 7, the eve of the peace negotiations in Moscow. At the request of Finland the Administration offered to do what it could for the Finns without involving the United States in the discussions. Steinhardt saw Molotov again, and this time found him in a good humor. The Commissar was "effusively cordial" and willingly outlined the Soviet proposals to the Ambassador. Steinhardt intimated that were the terms lenient, the moral embargo might be lifted, but no agreement was reached by the two diplomats.[4] This was the full extent of the American aid in framing the peace. On March 13, the War ended. In recognizing this fact, Roosevelt issued a statement in which he proclaimed that:

> The people of Finland, by their unexcelled valor and strong resistance in the face of overwhelming armed forces, have won the moral right to live in everlasting peace and independence in the land which they have so bravely defended.[5]

Just prior to the signing of the treaty, most Americans believed the War would continue indefinitely. Judging by the newspapers it would seem that the United States thought that the Finns could resist the Soviet attacks. News of Soviet victories began to circulate in the middle of February, but these stories were usually followed by accounts of successful Finnish counterattacks. This type of reporting continued almost to the end of the War. "You may read today of the Russian capture of Viborg," wrote one reporter on March 4, "and within 10 days or a fortnight you may hear that the Red Army has marched into Helsinki."

> That, you may say, is a crushing blow for the Finnish Army, but you will be wrong. . . . Although the Finnish Army may retreat . . . the Army will fight on![6]

The realization that Finland had lost the War came as a shock to the American people. Most were surprised on that morning of March 13. The Mannerheim Line was holding, as were the forces in other parts of Finland. Why then did the Helsinki Government capitulate? To the average American the obvious answer was that Finland had failed diplomatically even though she had succeeded militarily. She had not been able to receive the necessary aid from Scandinavia, Great Britain, France and the United States. As the public searched Europe for a scapegoat, the press reminded them that the Administration and Congress had done little to aid the Finns. "Americans have scant right to cast a stone at any other democracy" was the verdict of one newspaper.

> The tardiness with which Congress acted and the hesitation widely displayed toward assuming the slightest risk in the situation were hardly determining factors at first. They are not, however, accomplishments of which this country can be proud.[7]

The *New York Times* cautioned against placing the blame on friendly European powers, whose situations might not be fully appreciated on this side of the Atlantic. "In any case," it editorialized, "there is no justification for anyone, least of all those far removed from the danger zone, to point an accusing finger at either the Allied powers or at Scandinavia." [8]

Many Americans were conscience-stricken in much the same fashion as other western nations which had expressed sympathy for Finland. Much had been said during the Russo-Finnish War; little had been done. Some Americans attempted to aid Finland after the War in order to expiate the sins of omission committed during the fighting. General O'Ryan announced that Fighting Funds for Finland would continue its operations by collecting money to be used in the rehabilitation of Finnish military personnel, while Jesse Jones indicated that the

Finns could still draw upon the Export-Import Bank loan even though the fighting was over.[9] Senator Clark of Idaho introduced a measure in the upper house which would have placed that body on record as favoring the severance of relations with the U.S.S.R. Senator Brown, who had fashioned a national reputation during the War, announced that he would personally aid Finnish relief and advocated an additional loan of $20 million to Finland.[10] The Mayor of San Antonio, the redoubtable Maury Maverick, suggested to Roosevelt that the Administration invite all Finns who so desired to settle in Alaska at American expense.[11] In all, the pro-Finnish sentiment evoked by the War was retained by the American people. The Finns might have lost the last battle, wrote one national magazine, but their courage had earned them a place in "the company of Heroes of All Time, whose glory does not fade." [12]

During the last week of March the headlines were dominated by news of threatened German invasions in Scandinavia, artillery duels along the Maginot Line, labor legislation, and most of all, by the question of whether or not Roosevelt would run for a third term. By this time the Winter War was all but forgotten by the fickle American press; the public had turned its attention to new problems.[13]

From the viewpoint of the American people, the War had been an exciting episode which had enabled them to release some of their pent-up anti-totalitarian feelings. Supporting Finland and opposing Communism had been harmless enough. There was no danger of a Soviet-American conflict in 1939-40. Similar sympathies were felt for the Allies, but many seemed uneasy about joining French and British relief organizations. After all, wasn't that the way London and Paris had begun their campaign to drag the United States into the first World War?

The Winter War lasted little more than three months —a long time for Americans to remain at fever pitch over an issue which apparently had little direct effect on their personal fortunes. Indeed, the Hoover and O'Ryan appeals had almost disappeared from the newspapers by early February, and the war news received nowhere near the coverage it had been given in December. By March, one got the impression that the public had become bored with Finland's problems. Ending when it did, the War lasted just long enough for Americans to praise Finland and hiss the Soviets.

Soviet-American relations reached their nadir during the War. When the Red Army executed bloodless coups in the Baltic states in June, the United States retaliated by freezing the funds of those nations which had been deposited in American banks. Sumner Welles had tried to achieve better relations with the Soviet leaders, in many cases bypassing Hull, much to the chagrin of the Secretary, who would have preferred working through regular diplomatic channels. In July, Welles held conversations with Oumansky in an attempt to check the deteriorating situation which had developed between Washington and Moscow.[14] The episode of the Baltic funds led the Soviet statesman to protest to the Under Secretary, who proceeded to forget his position in the heat of argument and told Oumansky that the United States recognized no difference between the aggressions of the Soviet Union and those of Nazi Germany.[15]

In an address before the Supreme Soviet on August 1, Molotov bluntly indicated that all was not well between his nation and the United States. "I will not dwell on our relations with the United States of America," he told the delegates, "if only for the reason that there is nothing good that can be said about them."[16] Nevertheless, on August 6, the Soviet-American trade agreement was renewed with little trouble. This was the one bright spot in the relations between the two countries in this period. Indeed, commerce between the Soviet Union and the United States increased greatly in 1940. The total value of this trade far exceeded that for 1939, in spite of the moral embargo and the general deterioration of diplomatic relations.[17]

Faced with the common danger of Nazi Germany, Roosevelt and Stalin seemed to realize that they had one important policy in common: opposition to Axis expansion. In an atmosphere of pure opportunism, Soviet-American relations slowly began to improve. The American people, however, could not as easily forget a generation of anti-Soviet sentiments, which had been heightened and epitomized by the Russo-Finnish War. For more than a year after the War had ended many Americans were still convinced that the only course Roosevelt could rightly follow would be that of severing relations with the Soviet Union. Even after the German attack on the Soviet Union in 1941, a group remained which pleaded with the public to remember that despite this new development in the World War, the major enemy of democracy was the U.S.S.R. Colonel Robert McCormick, the apostle of midwestern isolationism, was the most ardent exponent of this point of view. He constantly repeated the same theme:

> I would a hundred times rather see my country ally herself with England, or even with Germany with all her faults, than with the cruelty, the godlessness, and the barbarism that exists in Soviet Russia.[18]

In January of 1941, as the Nazi plans for the invasion of the Soviet Union were being mapped out, Welles made another attempt at *rapproachment*. Calling Oumansky to his offices, he told the Ambassador that the State Department had definite information to the effect that the German invasion would take place the following June. Although Oumansky made no attempt to pursue the matter, this conversation was reported to Moscow. At the same time, the two nations signified their common aims by agreeing informally to work toward the maintenance of the *status quo* in the Far East. A common enemy, Japan, united the Soviets and Americans in that part of the world as Hitler had in Europe. Another manifestation of the Soviet leaders' concern with American relations came after the German occupation of Bulgaria, when the United States was assured by Moscow that the U.S.S.R. disapproved of the action. A new era in the history of Soviet-American relations opened on January 21, when Roosevelt lifted the moral embargo against the Soviet Union.[19] By the summer of 1941 the two nations were still "separated by an ideological gulf," which was, however, being "joined by a bridge of national interest."[20]

Relations with Finland were maintained on the same plane as during the War. The O'Ryan drive and the various aid bills pending in Congress died quietly, however, as America's interest and attention was turned elsewhere. The Finnish Government engaged itself in extensive rehabilitation and the resettlement of those whose farms had become Soviet territory as a result of peace treaty.[21] The Hoover funds were used to great advantage in this work. The Soumen Huolto—the Finnish Agency for Relief—found itself in the pleasant situation of having more resources than it could use. By June, 165,678,144:10 marks remained to be spent or earmarked for projects. During the three months after the peace had been signed the Soumen Huolto made most of its grants to regional groups and to hospitals.[22] But despite this aid from American donors and the Scandinavian states, the Finns did not look to the West for assistance. Geography had doomed her to act as a buffer between Germany and the Soviet Union, and the Winter War caused Helsinki to turn to Berlin. There was an unquestionable desire on the part of most Finns for *revanche,* and when Germany attacked the Soviet Union on June 22, Finland was at her side.

This presented a problem to the American people and their Government. Much had transpired since March of 1940. The destroyer deal with Great Britain, lend-lease, the introduction of conscription, and the increased military budget—all were indicative of a growing American adherence to the Allied cause. By mid-1941 there were few Americans who doubted that their country would have to play a role of some kind in the European struggle.[23] By that time Stalin was fighting side by side with Churchill, who had severed relations with Hitler's ally, Finland. This was the development that Roosevelt and Hull had hoped for in 1939-1940, and what Welles had expected in January of 1941.

The American Government now tried to draw Finland out of the war. That nation still maintained a reservoir of good will in the United States and, in addition, there were important military considerations to be dealt with. By October the Finnish Army under Mannerheim was battering down the gates of Leningrad; the vital rail link with Murmansk was almost closed by advance units of the Finnish Army.

As early as August 18, Welles had sounded out Procope as to the possibility of a Russo-Finnish peace and eventual alliance. He informed the Finnish Ambassador that Stalin was willing to make a territorial adjustment. Understandably wary of Soviet intentions, Procope demanded that any agreement that his country might enter into with the Soviets be guaranteed by Great Britain and the United States. After all, what assurances had Helsinki that the Soviets would carry out their part of the bargain? Welles was not prepared to accept the Finnish conditions, and later wrote:

> What guarantees or assurances Finland thought she would have of retaining her own independence and autonomy if Germany . . . were the overlord of all Europe. I said that in such an event Finland could look to no one for assistance whereas if Germany were defeated she would have extremely powerful friends on her side.[24]

This type of argument failed to satisfy Helsinki. After the August meeting Finnish-American relations began to deteriorate, reaching a low point in November, when Finland joined the anti-Comintern pact. With this action relations reached the breaking point. Conditions were further complicated when the United States entered the war in December. Although Congress never declared war on Finland, that nation was now, in effect, the enemy of the United States. Procope was amazed at this rapid turnabout. From her lofty position of esteem in 1939, Finland had fallen to a point where she was coupled with Hitler and Mussolini as an enemy of the West.

In 1941, as the Germans poised for the eventual blow in the East, the Soviet Union's relations with the Allies became far closer than ever before, and the American Government also began to moderate its attitude toward the Stalin dictatorship. This was to mark the beginning of a revolution in Soviet-American relations, which was to lead to the apogee of friendship and sympathy in 1943-1944, when news of Soviet victories and the heroism of the Russian people were on everyone's lips. Finland, on the other hand, had allied herself with Hitler, and the Nazis were to be offered no mercy by either the West or the Soviet Union. Under these circumstances what would be the fate of Finland in case of an Allied victory? Those Americans who thought of the situation found it difficult to place men like Mannerheim in the same catogory as Hitler and Tojo. But the truth of the matter is that few considered the question; the issue of Finnish-American relations was lost in the greater problems of preserving the western world from totalitarianism. There were some who remembered the Russo-Finnish War at the time that Finland joined the Axis partnership. "We yield to nobody in our dislike for Hitler or in our hope to see him someday, somehow, kicked up some convenient blind alley for good," wrote *Collier's* after the German attack on the Soviet Union.

> Nevertheless we have to stretch our imaginations strenuously in order to picture ourselves hating Finland. . . . Finland gagged for a few days but finally sided with Hitler. To repeat, we don't blame Finland. . . . We also hope that Finland may somehow come out of this fight stronger, better protected, and happier than ever before.[25]

In September of 1941, Hull called on Procope in another attempt to draw Finland out of the German orbit. The United States exerted considerable pressure on Helsinki toward this end, warning the Finns that any gains she might make in the early stages of the new war would be wiped out once the Nazis were defeated. However, at that time the German advances in the Soviet Union had convinced the Finns that they had picked the winning side, and they were not responsive to Hull's entreaties. As a result Finnish-American relations became progressively worse. On October 26 and 28, Hull sent the Helsinki Government notes which were "so strong that they fell short of a breach of relations." At the same time "our relations with Russia became even closer in the autumn of 1941."[26] The die was cast; Finland was to be considered a full member of the Axis, while her enemy, the U.S.S.R., would be treated as a co-equal member of the Allies.

The wave of pro-Finnish sentiment which had engulfed the nation during the winter of 1939-1940 was forgotten by 1944, as was much of the anti-Soviet sentiment of that period. At Yalta, Stalin alluded to Finland and asserted that the Soviet Union should have the deciding vote as to her fate.

> My colleagues in Moscow cannot forget what happened in December, 1939, during the Russo-Finnish War, when the British and French used the League of Nations against us and succeeded in isolating and expelling the Soviet Union from the League, and when they later mobilized against us and talked of a crusade against Russia.[27]

Stalin insisted that Soviet security could be had only by making Finland a satellite. By this time the United States had lost interest in Finland, and as a result the Soviet Union was given a large say in the destiny of her northern neighbor.[28]

The old cliches about yesterday's friends being today's enemies, war making strange bedfellows, and time instituting great changes, might easily have been applied to the Finnish situation. The payment of the debts, the Russo-Finnish War, twenty years of excellent relations —all were largely forgotten or obscured by 1945. At that time Finland occupied a position on the American conscience which her size and position should have dictated from the first. The average American knew of Finland, but he also knew of Roumania and Bulgaria, and all were lumped together as minor accomplices of Hitler and Mussolini. This, a secondary result of five years of World War.

NOTES

Chapter X: THE AFTERMATH

1 Wourinen, *Finland and World War II,* p. 74 ff.

2 Dallin, *Soviet Russia's Foreign Policy,* p. 187; Mannerheim, *Memoirs,* p. 364; Langer and Gleason, *Challenge to Isolation,* p. 399.

3 Langer and Gleason, *Challenge to Isolation,* p. 398.

4 Hull, *Memoirs,* Vol. II, p. 742.

5 *New York Times,* March 14, 1940.

6 Courtney Tennett in *New York Journal and American,* March 4, 1940.

7 *New York Herald Tribune,* March 13, 1940.

8 *New York Times,* March 13, 1940.

9 *Newsweek* (Vol. 15, No. 12, March 25, 1940), p. 16.

10 *New York World Telegram,* March 15, 1940.

11 Telegram from Maverick to Roosevelt, March 22, 1940, in *Roosevelt Papers.* On March 16, Brazil has announced that she would admit 100,000 additional Finnish immigrants. See *The United States in World Affairs,* 1940, p. 358.

12 "What the Finns Won" (*Collier's* Vol. 105, No. 15, April 13, 1940), p. 82.

13 This is based on a survey of twenty-four leading daily newspapers. See *Bibliography.*

14 Sumner Welles, *The Time for Decision* (New York, 1944), pp. 169-70.

15 Langer and Gleason, *Challenge to Isolation,* p. 646.

16 *Christian Science Monitor,* August 2, 1940.

17 Trade in selected items was:

Item	*1939*	*1940 (9 months)*
Machine Tools	$18 628 384	$19 399 698
Non-Ferrous Metals	8 395 621	19 240 045
Petroleum Products	1 172 118	996 680

Total trade in 1939 was $51,808,490. This figure was surpassed during the first nine months of 1940, when trade totalled $58,524,000. See *Business Week* (No. 583, November 2, 1940), p. 60.

18 *Chicago Tribune,* June 25, 1941.

19 Davis and Lindley, *How War Came,* pp. 175-78.

20 Walter Lippman in *Ibid.,* p. 245.

21 Axel De Gadolin, *The Solution of the Karelian Refugee Problem in Finland* (The Hague, 1952).

22 *Finnish Relief Fund Report,* p. 25 ff.

23 The best treatment of this subject is Wayne Cole, *America First: The Battle Against Intervention* (Madison, 1953).

24 Davis and Lindley, *How War Came,* p. 280.

25 "We Still Like Finland" (*Collier's* Vol. 108, No. 5, August 2, 1941), p. 54.

26 Hull, *Memoirs,* Vol. II, p. 980.

27 Winston Churchill, *Triumph and Tragedy* (New York, 1949), p. 358.

28 Byrnes, *Speaking Frankly,* pp. 102-3, 111-12, 148, 154.

Chapter XI

CONCLUSION

The subject of this study is the metamorphosis of American attitudes toward foreign affairs during the winter of 1939-1940. During this period the basic positions of isolationist and internationalist were examined, attacked, found wanting and, to a degree, discarded.

The isolationists were under attack in 1939, and the events in Europe caused them to beat a retreat. By November they found themselves in the process of surrendering their majority status in the determination of American foreign policy. They tried to keep the nation neutral, but early in the conflict they were faced with a difficult situation. Should aid be given the Allies, thus preventing an Axis victory, the action might draw the United States into the war. On the other hand, refusal to grant such help might lead to a German victory and a subsequent attempt on the part of Hitler to conquer the western hemisphere.

From the first, inheritance and ideology contributed toward enlisting the emotions of the majority of Americans in the Allied cause. Those isolationists who did not take cognizance of this lost much of their following. The former isolationists could not accept Wilsonian internationalism as espoused by Hull; they considered the doctrine inadequate. Neither position seemed to answer the pressing needs of American foreign policy in 1939. As a result, both ossified and eventually declined or changed.

Their places at the poles of American attitudes in foreign affairs were taken by interventionists and non-interventionists. The former believed that the United States must take an active part in aiding the Allies. The title of their most important organization—the Committee to Defend America by Aiding the Allies—is self-explanatory. Most of those who held this belief thought that the crisis would be temporary, and that after it passed the old categories would again come to the fore. Although many internationalists became interventionists, there is no positive correlation between the two attitudes. Many isolationists joined the White Committee in the belief that by so acting they would eradicate a temporary menace to American security, after which they could retire once more behind the Atlantic and Pacific Oceans and Washington's farewell address. Some internationalists—such as Chester Bowles and Robert Hutchins—joined the leading non-interventionist organization—America First—in the belief that Britain and France could win the war without American aid.

As these important questions were discussed in the most important foreign policy debate in a generation, Germany and the Soviet Union carved eastern Europe into spheres of influence. Stalin was given Finland as part of his portion, and after a whirlwind diplomatic campaign in the Baltic, that nation was approached by Soviet emissaries who attempted to draw Premier Erkko into the Soviet sphere of influence. Threats and promises proved useless, and on the last day of November the Russo-Finnish War began. It was a small war as European wars go, and most "inside observers" thought that it would end in a Soviet victory within a few weeks. But the Finns proved to be tougher than had been expected, while the Red Army did not exert its full military might in the beginning. The War dragged on for three and a half months, and during this period the United States was forced to make moral and political decisions of grave importance which changed the nature of the foreign policy debate.

The isolationists had vented their spleen at Great Britain and France, while the non-interventionists stated that these two nations did not deserve nor need American help in World War II. Both disregarded Finland in the formulation of their philosophies. The Finns had an excellent reputation in the United States, and Finland was considered one of the foremost friends of this country in Europe. Therefore, when she was attacked by the Soviet Union, the stage was set for official and unofficial action in Finland's behalf. Roosevelt had many weapons in his arsenal to carry through such a program. Since Finland had always paid her debts, she was not prevented by the Johnson Act from obtaining private credits in the United States. The burdensome arms embargo of the Neutrality Act had been repealed at the special session, so that loans and credits could be used to purchase munitions and other implements of war. The only drawback was the cash-and-carry provision which, designed to aid the Allies, operated to the detriment of the Finns. It was possible, however, considering the British position toward the War, for Allied vessels to be used in the Finnish cause. Had the interventionists desired, such a program could easily have been carried through.

This course of action was given scant consideration. Instead, the American people and their representatives hesitated, and then refused to grant military credits. Interventionists, considering the British and French cause to be more important than that of Finland, observed that such an action would alienate the Soviet Union from the West, and eventually serve to make Stalin a full partner in the Axis. The Administration could not act in view of the broader significance of the European conflict. Congress, fearful of the effects of a bold move, and yet also aware of public support for aid to Finland, passed the mild Brown Bill after a lengthy and unseemly debate. 1940 was to be an election year, the most important election year in regard to foreign policy since 1916, and Roosevelt, who had begun his move toward interventionism, and the majority of congressmen, who were divided as to which course of action to take, acted in a most cautious manner. The public, lacking strong leadership and misled by the press, had its energies drawn off by the Hoover Fund and similar organizations which did not provide Finland with the military aid she so desperately needed.

The War was important to the United States in that it constituted an invaluable lesson in international relations and power politics. Since the "Nye mentality" could not be utilized in regard to Finland, the isolationists were robbed of their most important weapon. The public was free to discuss the War, to advocate aid to Finland and to dislike the Soviets, without being reminded that the salesmen of death, the cunning British and French foreign offices, and the lobbyists, were behind the Finnish cause. The non-interventionists, who had concentrated on opposing European wars as none of the United States' business, were confused and split by the Russo-

Finnish War. They had opposed Britain, France, and the Soviet Union as representatives of those forces which would involve Americans in wars which were none of their immediate concern, while Hitler and Mussolini were despised because of their obvious anti-democratic methods and aims. But the Finns represented Democracy, and should not American aid be granted to a nation which stood alone against totalitarian aggression? The special circumstances of the War enlisted many non-interventionists in pro-Finnish causes. Interventionists opposed aid to Finland—in private, of course—arguing that this would detract from the movement to aid the Allies. Thus, the interventionists opposed aid to Finland, while many non-interventionists argued for a measure of American interest in the Winter War. By the time the War had ended, the non-interventionists' position was hopelessly compromised. If the United States should practice the policy of "America First," how does one justify pro-Finnish sentiments and actions? Their inability to answer this question, combined with further developments in the European situation, served to undermine and eventually cripple the non-interventionist position. The interventionists, on the other hand, simply turned their attentions from the Russo-Finnish War in March, and once again agitated for American aid to France and Britain.

As early as February 14, 1940, Walter Millis began to change many of his ideas about American foreign affairs. On this date he issued a plea asking Americans to "begin thinking a little less exclusively about the last war" and to start thinking "a little more imaginatively about the present one."[1] Millis had been an isolationist who had converted to interventionism. Earlier in the month, Vandenberg, who by that time had emerged as the foreign policy spokesman of the Republican Party, admitted to himself that isolationism was not in tune with the times. He struggled to twist that doctrine into a more acceptable and up-to-date form. "It is probably impossible," he wrote in his diary, "that there should be such a thing as old fashioned isolation in this present foreshortened world when one can cross the Atlantic Ocean in 36 hours." He still hoped that the water barrier would remain the nation's first line of defense.

> But probably the best we can hope for from now on is "insulation" rather than isolation. I should say that an "insulationist" is one who wants to preserve all of the isolation which modern circumstances will permit.[2]

Vandenberg was an isolationist whose "insulationism" was close to interventionism. Like Millis, he was a non-interventionist when the World War began, and like Millis, he began his turn to interventionism during the Russo-Finnish War.[3]

Americans turned from isolationism unwillingly when the World War came to Europe. The abortive attempt to substitute in its place the doctrine of non-interventionism was shown to be all but impossible during the Russo-Finnish War. Today both doctrines are minority sentiments. Senator Taft, leader of the Republican Party in Congress after Vandenberg's death, said in 1950 that "only an idiot would be an isolationist today,"[4] while President-elect Eisenhower, in one of his first statements after the 1952 elections, told the American people that "isolationism in America is dead as a political issue."[5]

Attitudes toward foreign affairs following World War I were not duplicated after the second conflict. There were few responsible observers such as the Millis of the thirties who would speak for non-interventionists of the forties and fifties. Nor were there Gerald Nyes or Bennett Clarks in the Senate. C. C. Tansill and Charles Beard spoke for a group of historians who constituted themselves as a "revisionist" school after World War II, but neither received the hearing of their predecessors after World War I. During the twenties, Beard was looked upon as the prophet of the "New History," and achieved great fame not only among historians but with the general public as well. This success was not duplicated after World War II. Senator McCarthy had more power than Vandenberg, Borah, Johnson, and Nye, but few would claim that he was as representative as the Administration critics after World War I. In attacking "Merchants of Death," Nye appealed to the mass of Americans in an isolationist climate of opinion. In attacking Roosevelt's actions at Yalta, McCarthy spoke forcefully, but to a smaller audience who lived in an interventionist climate of opinion. Isolationist Vandenberg stood a good chance of gaining the Republican nomination in 1940, since it was felt that he could appeal to a majority of Americans.[6] McCarthy's hopes for the Republican nomination at the height of his power were all but non-existent.

The major reason for this was the lack of a strong isolationist sentiment in the United States after World War II. That doctrine was stopped by the German attack on Poland, and turned back with the Soviet attack on Finland. The Russo-Finnish War was not the most important event in this change, but it was an important milestone in the turn to interventionism. For a few weeks it aroused the United States as much as the invasion of Belgium did in World War I, and as such, must be considered significant.

There is one other facet of the war which merits consideration. The Soviet attack was the last important matter to be considered by the League of Nations. At the time, the world organization was a mere shell of what it had been in the twenties, and even then it did not resemble the Wilsonian dream of 1919. As the League met to deliberate the case, Stalin sent the following message to the Finnish people:

> The Red Army is approaching Finland's borders at the request of the Finnish People's Government. As soon as the People's Government requests it, it will leave Finnish territory. The Red Army is going into Finland to aid the Finnish people . . . to secure Finnish independence . . . to establish *friendly relations* with Finland.[7]

The League recommended economic sanctions against the U.S.S.R. and that nation retaliated by leaving the world organization. In all, the actions of the Geneva diplomats had little effect on the course of the War.

More than a decade later, the Communist regime of China intervened in the Korean War, and the messages sent to the people of that nation were remarkably similar in tone and content to those issued by the Kremlin in December of 1939. They too were coming as "good neighbors." Where the Soviets aided Otto Kuusinen's puppet government, the Chinese were to buttress the shaky North Korean regime. This time the situation was far different than it was in 1939; this aggression was met by an international force which fought under the United Nations flag—which aided Korea in a manner which, had it been applied to Finland in 1939, would have changed the course of history. Leading the U.N. forces was the United States, defending with military might a nation which was further from San Francisco than Finland was from New York.

NOTES

Chapter XI: CONCLUSION

1 *New York Herald Tribune,* February 14, 1940.

2 Arthur H. Vandenberg, Jr., ed., *The Private Papers of Senator Vandenberg* (Boston, 1952), pp. 3-4.

3 This movement in the direction of interventionism was completed when, after the Pearl Harbor attack, Vandenberg wrote: "My convictions regarding international cooperation and collective security for peace took form on the afternoon of the Pearl Harbor attack. That day ended isolationism for any realist." *Ibid,* p. 1.

4 Dulles, *America's Rise to World Power,* p. 244.

5 *New York Times,* September 10, 1952.

6 *Newsweek* (Vol. 15, No. 101, March 4, 1940), p. 10.

7 Dallin, *Soviet Russia's Foreign Policy,* p. 141.

BIBLIOGRAPHY

MANUSCRIPTS

Roosevelt Papers. The public and private papers of Franklin D. Roosevelt are on deposit at the Franklin D. Roosevelt Library at Hyde Park, New York. Those messages and memoranda relating to the Russo-Finnish War have not as yet been catalogued. The documents relating to the war itself and the messages received by the President are included in five file boxes.

PERIODICALS

American Journal of International Law
American Mercury
American Political Science Review
Atlantic Monthly
Bulletin of International News
Business Week
Christian Century
Collier's
Common Sense
Congressional Digest
Current History
Editor and Publisher
Foreign Affairs
Fortune
Harper's
Keep America Out of War Congress Record
Life
Literary Digest
Living Age

Nation
New Masses
New Republic
Newsweek
Political Science Quarterly
Public Opinion Quarterly
Saturday Evening Post
Scholastic
Speech Monographs
Time
U.S. News and World Report
Vital Speeches
World Politics

NEWSPAPERS

Atlanta Constitution
Boston Globe
Chicago Daily News
Chicago Tribune
Christian Science Monitor
Cincinnati Enquirer
Daily Worker
Dallas Morning News
London Times
Los Angeles Times
Louisville Courier-Journal
Milwaukee Journal
New York Daily News
New York Herald Tribune
New York Journal and American
New York Post
New York Times
New York World Telegram
Portland Oregonian
Progressive
Socialist Call
Wall Street Journal
Washington Daily News
Washington Evening Star

BOOKS

Adler, Selig. *The Isolationist Impulse.* New York, 1957.
Alsop, Joseph and Kintner, Robert. *American White Paper.* New York, 1940.

Anonymous. *The Mirrors of Washington.* New York, 1921.

Bailey, Thomas A. *The Man in the Street.* New York, 1948.

Baker, Newton D. *Why We Went to War.* New York, 1936.

Baker, Roscoe. *The American Legion and American Foreign Policy.* New York, 1954.

Barnes, Harry E. editor. *Perpetual War for Perpetual Peace.* New York, 1952.

Beard, Charles A. *American Foreign Policy in the Making: 1932-1940.* New Haven, 1946.

.... *The Devil Theory of War.* New York, 1936.

.................., and Mary R. *America in Midpassage.* New York, 1942.

.... *The American Spirit.* New York, 1942.

Belmont, Perry. *National Isolation as an Illusion.* New York, 1925.

Borah, William E. *Bedrock.* Washington, 1936.

Borchard, Edwin and Lage, William P. *Neutrality for the United States.* New Haven, 1940.

Browder, Robert P. *Origins of Soviet-American Diplomacy.* Princeton, 1953.

Buell, Raymond L. *Isolated America.* New York, 1940.

Byrnes, James. *All in One Lifetime,* New York, 1958.

Cantril, Hadley. editor. *Public Opinion, 1935-1946.* Princeton, 1953.

Carter, Boake. *Why Meddle in Europe,* New York, 1939.

Chamberlin, William H. *America's Second Crusade.* Chicago, 1950.

Cole, Wayne C. *America First—The Battle Against In-*

tervention, 1940-1941. Madison, Wisconsin, 1953.

Coughlin, Charles. *Why Leave Our Own?* Detroit, 1939.

Curti, Merle. *The American Peace Crusade.* New York, 1929.

Davies, Joseph E. *Mission to Moscow.* New York, 1941.

Davis, Forrest and Lindley, Ernest K. *How War Came.* New York, 1942.

Drummond, Donald F. *The Passing of American Neutrality.* Ann Arbor, 1955.

Dulles, Foster Rhea. *America's Rise to World Power.* New York, 1955.

.... *The Road to Teheran.* New York, 1947.

Eliot, George Fielding. *The Ramparts We Watch.* New York, 1939.

Englebrecht, H. C. and Hanighen, F. C. *The Merchants of Death.* New York, 1934.

Farley, James. *Behind the Ballots.* New York, 1936.

Fenwick, Charles C. *American Neutrality: Trial and Failure.* New York, 1940.

Flynn, John T. *The Roosevelt Myth.* New York, 1948.

Frank, Jerome. *Save America First.* New York, 1938.

Freidel, Frank. *Franklin D. Roosevelt: The Ordeal.* Boston, 1954.

Goldman, Albert. *Why We Defend the Soviet Union.* New York, 1940.

Goldman, Eric. *Rendezvous With Destiny.* New York, 1952.

Graebner, Norman A. *The New Isolationism: A Study in Politics and Foreign Policy Since 1950.* New York, 1956.

Grassmuck, George L. *Sectional Biases in Congress on Foreign Policy* (The Johns Hopkins University Series in Historical and Political Science, Series LXVIII, Number 3). Baltimore, 1951.

Grattan, C. Hartley. *The Deadly Parallel.* New York, 1939.

Gunther, John. *Roosevelt in Retrospect.* New York, 1950.

Hartz, Louis. *The Liberal Tradition in America.* New York, 1955.

Herring, Hubert. *And So to War.* New Haven, 1938.

Hicks, Granville. *Where We Came Out.* New York, 1954.

Hinton, Harold. *Cordell Hull: A Biography.* New York, 1942.

Hooker, Nancy Harvison. editor. *The Moffat Papers.* Cambridge, Massachusetts, 1956.

Howe, Quincy. *Blood is Cheaper than Water.* New York, 1939.

Hull, Cordell. *The Memoirs of Cordell Hull.* 2 volumes. New York, 1948.

Ickes, Harold. *The Secret Diary of Harold Ickes.* 3 volumes. New York, 1954.

Johnson, Claudius O., *Borah of Idaho.* New York, 1936.

Johnson, Walter. *The Battle Against Isolation.* Chicago, 1944.

Jones, S. Shepard and Myers, Denys P. editors. *Documents on American Foreign Relations, January, 1938-June, 1939.* Boston, 1939.

Langer, William L. and Gleason, S. Everett. *The Challenge to Isolation, 1937-1940.* New York, 1952.

Lovenstein, Meno. *American Opinion of Soviet Russia.* Washington, 1941.

Lubell, Samuel. *The Future of American Politics.* New York, 1952.

Lyons, Eugene. *The Red Decade.* New York, 1941.

MacDougall, Curtis D. *Understanding Public Opinion.* New York, 1952.

Manley, Chesly. *The Twenty Year Revolution from Roosevelt to Eisenhower.* Chicago, 1954.

Millis, Walter. *The Roard to War.* New York, 1935.

Moley, Raymond. *After Seven Years.* New York, 1939.

Morrissey, Alice M. *American Defense of Neutral Rights.* Boston, 1939.

Moulton, Harold G. and Pasvolsky, Leo. *War Debts and World Prosperity.* Washington, 1932.

Peterson, H. C. *Propaganda For War: The Campaign Against American Neutrality, 1914-1917.* Norman, Oklahoma, 1939.

Rauch, Basil. *Roosevelt From Munich to Pearl Harbor.* New York, 1950.

Rippy, J. Fred. *America and the Strife of Europe.* New York, 1938.

Robinson, Edgar E. *The Roosevelt Leadership, 1933-1945.* New York, 1955.

.... *They Voted for Roosevelt.* Stanford, 1947.

Roosevelt, Elliott. editor. *F.D.R: His Personal Letters.* 3 volumes. New York, 1950.

Roosevelt, Franklin D. *Roosevelt's Foreign Policy, 1933-1941.* New York, 1942.

The Public Papers and Addresses of Franklin D. Roosevelt. New York, 1938-1950.

Schlesinger, Arthur M. Jr. *The Age of Roosevelt: The Crisis of the Old Order.* Boston, 1957.

Seymour, Charles. *American Diplomacy During the World War.* Baltimore, 1934.

Shepardson, Whitney H. and Scroogs, William O. editors. *The United States in World Affairs, 1939.* New York, 1940.

.... *The United States in World Affairs, 1940.* New York, 1941.

Sherwood, Robert. *Roosevelt and Hopkins.* New York, 1948.

Simonds, Frank H. *Can America Stay at Home?* New York, 1932.

Smith, Denys. *America and the Axis War.* London, 1942.

Stimson, Henry L. and Bundy, McGeorge. *On Active Service in Peace and War.* New York, 1948.

Tansill, Charles C. *America Goes to War.* New York, 1938.

.... *Back Door to War—The Roosevelt Foreign Policy, 1933-1939.* Chicago, 1952.

Tucker, Ray and Barkley, Frederick A. *Sons of the Wild Jackass.* Boston, 1932.

Vandenberg, Arthur H. Jr. *The Private Papers of Senator Vandenberg.* Boston, 1952.

Welles, Sumner. *The Time for Decision.* New York, 1940.

ARTICLES

Adler, Selig. "Isolationism Since 1914." *American Scholar,* Vol. 21, Summer, 1952, 335-344.

Billington, Ray Allen. "The Origins of Middle Western Isolationism." *Political Science Quarterly.* Vol. 60, March, 1945, 44-64.

Bliven, Bruce. "This is Where I Came In." *New Republic,* Vol. 93, January 5, 1938, 245-246.

Borah, William E. "The Embargo and European Power Politics." *Vital Speeches,* Vol. 6, October 15, 1939, 21-23.

Brandenburg, Ernest. "Franklin D. Roosevelt's International Speeches 1939-1941." *Speech Monographs,* Vol. 16, No. 1, August, 1949, 39-41.

Brown, John Crosby. "American Isolationism." *Foreign Affairs,* Vol. 18, No. 1, October, 1939, 29-44.

Bullitt, William C. "How We Won the War and Lost the Peace." *Life,* Vol. 25, No. 9, August 30, 1948, 83-97.

Del, Robert. "Phil LaFollette is Right." *Nation,* Vol. 148, No. 18, April 29, 1939, 487-488.

Denney, George V. Jr. "What's Your Opinion?" *Current History,* Vol. 51, No. 2, October, 1939, 42-46.

Dulles, Allen W. "Cash and Carry Neutrality." *Foreign Affairs,* Vol. 18, No. 2, January, 1940, 179-195.

Eliot, George Fielding. "The Russian Campaign Against Finland." *Life,* Vol. 8, No. 3, January 15, 1940, 19-28.

Elliston, H. B. "On the Finnish Front." *Atlantic,* Vol. 165, No. 2, February, 1940, 243-249.

Editors of *Fortune.* "Arms and the Men." *Fortune,* Vol. 9, No. 3, March, 1934, 53-57, 113-126.

Galbraith, John K. "The Twisted History of Our 1930's." *Reporter,* Vol. 13, No. 2, August 11, 1955, 4-6.

Jacob, Philip E. "U.S. 'Neutrality' Opinion." *Public Opinion,* Vol. 4, No. 1, March, 1940, 48-65.

Johnson, Claudius O. "William E. Borah, the People's Choice." *Pacific Northwest Quarterly,* Vol. 44, No. 1, January, 1953, 15-22.

Leopold, Richard W. "The Mississippi Valley and American Foreign Policy, 1890-1941: An Assessment and an Appeal." *Mississippi Valley Historical Review,* Vol. 37, March, 1951, 625-641.

Lubell, Samuel. "Who Votes Isolationist and Why." *Harper's,* Vol. 202, No. 1211, April, 1951, 29-37.

Millis, Walter. "1939 is not 1914." *Life,* Vol. 7, November 6, 1939, 69ff.

Moore, John Bassett. "The New Isolation." *American Journal of International Law,* Vol. 27, No. 4, October, 1933, 607-629.

"The Morgenthau Diaries, Part III." *Collier's,* Vol. 120, No. 15, October 14, 1947, 20-22, 72-79.

Roosevelt, Franklin D. "Our Foreign Policy: A Democratic View." *Foreign Affairs,* Vol. 6, No. 4, July, 1928, 573-586.

Seldes, George. "The Art of News Faking." *New Masses,* Vol. 24, No. 5, January 23, 1940, 3-6.

Tait, Samuel W. Jr. "Champ Clark's Boy." *American Mercury,* Vol. 28, No. 109, January, 1933, 70-77.

Wickware, Francis S. "What We Think About Foreign Affairs." *Harper's,* Vol. 179, No. 987, September, 1939, 397-406.

Wienberg, Albert A. "The Historical Meaning of the American Doctrine of Isolation." *American Political Science Review,* Vol. 34, June, 1940, pp. 539-547.

Wilcox, Francis O. "American Government and Politics: The Neutrality Fight in Congress: 1939." *American Political Science Review,* Vol. 33, No. 5, October, 1939, 811-825.

PAMPHLETS

Cromwell, James. *Isolation Vs. Democracy.* Newark, New Jersey, 1939.

The Emergency Peace Crusade. *The No Foreign War Crusade.* Philadelphia, 1937.

Socialist Labor Party. *Stalinist International Anarchism.* New York, 1940.

GOVERNMENT PUBLICATIONS

Department of State. *Documents on German Foreign Policy, 1918-1945.* Series A-D. Washington, 1949-1950.

.... Raymond J. Sontag and James S. Beddie, editors. *Nazi-Soviet Relations.* Washington, 1948.

.... *Peace and War, United States Foreign Policy, 1931-1941.* Washington, 1943.

.... *Foreign Relations of the United States, The Soviet Union, 1933-1939.* Washington, 1943.

House of Representatives. Foreign Affairs Committee. 74th Congress, 1st Session. *On H.R. 7125 (To Prohibit the Making of Loans or the Extension of Credit to Any Nation Engaged in Armed Conflict, Unless the United States is Engaged in Such Conflict as the Ally of Such Nation.)* Washington, 1935.

—————— 75th Congress, 1st Session. *On H.J. Resolution 422 (To Prohibit Loans and Maintain the Neutrality of the United States in the Event of War or Threat of War Between or Among Foreign Nations.)* Washington, 1936.

—————— 76th Congress, 1st Session. *On the Present Neutrality Law (Public Resolution No. 27, 75th Congress.)* Washington, 1939.

—————— Committee on Banking and Currency 76th Congress, 3rd Session. *On S. 3069 (H.R. 8477) (A Bill to Provide for Increasing the Lending Authority of the Export-Import Bank of Washington, and for other Purposes.)* Washington, 1940.

Senate. Special Committee to Investigate the Munitions Industry. 73rd Congress, 1st Session. *Hearings Before the Special Committee Investigating the Munitions Industry.* Washington, 1934-1936.

—————— Foreign Relations Committee. 76th Congress, 1st Session. *Hearings Before the Committee on Foreign Relations.* Washington, 1939.

—————— 76th Congress, 3rd Session. *On S. 3069, A Bill to Provide for Certain Loans to the Republic of Finland by the Reconstruction Finance Corporation.* Washington, 1940.

Congressional Record. 73rd Congress—76th Congress, 1933-1940.

INDEX